OLD STONES

The
Biography
of a Family

TOUCHWOOD
EDITIONS

OLD STONES

The Biography of a Family

A. S. Penne

TouchWood Editions is an imprint of Horsdal & Schubart Publishers Ltd., Victoria, BC, Canada.
Distributed by The Heritage Group,
#108 – 17665 66A Avenue, Surrey, BC, Canada, V3S 2A7.

Cover design by Pat McCallum, layout by Katherine Hale, cover photo by Tania Strauss.

TouchWood Editions acknowledges the financial support for our publishing program from The Canada Council for the Arts, the Government of Canada through the Book Publishing Industry Development Program (BPDIP) and the Province of British Columbia through the British Columbia Arts Council.

This book is set in AGaramond.

Printed and bound in Canada by Transcontinental Printing.

National Library of Canada Cataloguing in Publication Data

Penne, A. S. (Anthea S.), 1951-
Old stones: the biography of a family / A.S. Penne.

ISBN 0-920663-85-0

1. Penne, A. S. (Anthea S.), 1951- 2. Penne family. 3. British Canadians—Biography. 4. Sechelt (B.C.)—Biography. I. Title.

FC3849.S42Z49 2002   971.1'3104'092   C2002-911014-9
F1089.5.S42P46 2002

Dedication

This book is for my mother and
in memory of my father (1923-2002).

Acknowledgments

I am indebted to Betty Keller for her longstanding efforts at bringing this book to print and to Edna Sheedy for her unfailing confidence in my abilities. For their continuous moral support, friendship and sometimes on-demand critiques, I thank Alys Howe and Anna Nobile. For their input at workshopping sessions, I am grateful to Jo Hammond (and husband Dick), Eve Smart and Dorothy Fraser. For her patience with my heel-digging, I also thank Vivian Sinclair. And finally, I am forever grateful to my parents for having the willingness and courage to share their personal stories, without which this manuscript would never have been written.

Contents

Home is where one starts from. As we grow older
The world becomes stranger, the pattern more complicated
Of dead and living. Not the intense moment
Isolated, with no before and after,
But a lifetime burning in every moment
And not the lifetime of one man only
But of old stones that cannot be deciphered.
— T.S. Eliot
from "East Coker"
(No. 2 of *Four Quartets*)

Prologue

A Foreign Language

*I*t began with my name.

My parents, Eric and Elizabeth, named me after their mothers, a time-honoured custom of the finest WASP tradition. And it must have been that my English grandmother was more in favour than the Canadian one at the time of my christening, because it is her name that has coloured my life.

When I was little, the usual reaction to my name would make me clam up, refuse to say it again. It was the audible surprise that always threw me, made me doubt my own existence.

"What *is it?*" they'd ask, eyes opening wide. Or, if they were Americans, "Say again?" And I'd frown or shrug, let my vision blur so I couldn't quite see their amazement. But I'd cry about it later, complain to my mother that she'd given me a weird name.

By the time I was a teenager, explaining my name had become a full-fledged performance and my adolescent friends rolled their eyes whenever they had to introduce me. Sometimes they gave my nickname — Annie — trying to avoid the questions that followed as inevitably as Vancouver's rain. Eventually I became protective of my heritage, proud of its uniqueness, and annoyed if I discovered someone else using it, someone with no idea of the history behind this family heirloom.

Anthea. I pronounce it slowly for new ears, moving my lips carefully so they can watch and copy me.

1

And the usual response: "Hi, Andrea — nice to meet you."
Then I smile patiently, suppressing the urge to sigh in exasperation.
"No," I say. "It's 'Anthea.' With a 'th' in the middle."
"Athena?"
"Not quite. Same letters, twisted around. A-N-T-H-E-A."
A slight pause.
"A-N-T-H ...?"
"E-A," I finish for them.
Some consternation.
"Well, that's a different one. Haven't heard that before. Anthe ...?"
"Anthea," I pronounce again.
I watch their lips move with effort as they feel the name on their palates. "Where's it from?" they ask, doubtful frowns on their brows. I can almost read their thoughts then: Why would someone give their child such a strange name? What's wrong with "Sue" or "Janet"?
Then inwardly I grimace, consider how much to tell them before shrugging. "It's an old family name. From my mother's mother."
"Oh?" Eyebrows raised. Must be some kind of foreigner.
"English," I explain, hoping to summarize in that one word all the twists and turns intestinal to the story. The subtle shades of family blood that have never homogenized, the nuances of foreignness that persist despite three generations of domestic wars on two continents.
But most people are on a different tack, wanting only to make conversation.
"What's your last name?" they ask hopefully. "Is it a different one too?"
And when I was young, I smirked in embarrassment, rolling my eyes heavenward in search of leniency. Unbelievable, to me, that my parents could have had the bad taste to combine such discordant names.
"Brown." Waiting for the laughter.
But first their heads shake from side to side, as if ashamed for me.
"Fancy first name, plain second name!" Upper-class aspirations, working-class reality.
And then my thoughts explode with a maelstrom of words begging to defend and explain. You don't understand, *I want to say. About the opposing realities of those two names and the force of their confused*

apposition. The not knowing which heritage to claim and the wishing I could be proud of both but wanting none of either.

This is where I have come from, where I have spent half my life. Searching for a place to call home despite a nagging feeling that I am without roots. This is how I came to be here, wading through the family archives. By daylight, now, I dream old lives into reality while at night, walking the dog under northern constellations, I search for my ancestors in the watery light above.

Seesawing through the memories, I begin to find my way home.

Coates Manor, Gloucestershire, England.

Belonging

Two doll-perfect faces look out of my parents' engagement photo, one with hair swept up in the fashionable waves and peaks of the time, the other with a wry smile, almost as if he knew what he was doing. These are the untainted versions of those same faces which today are wrinkle- and jowl-laden. If I thin the hair on Eric's head and thicken the eyebrows, I can see his lawyerly glare beneath the furrowed brow. But Elizabeth looks nothing like the old lady she has become.

The family backbone has always been a pride of pedigree, but a pedigree that varies according to which side of the Atlantic I am on. My father's people are Canadian pioneers, later the rough-around-the-edges working class of early Vancouver, and my mother's ancestors were English industrialists, landed gentry who depended on large battalions of servants to run outsized estates. These two extremes of culture, attitudes that have never successfully meshed, survive only to counter each other in an act that began with my parents' marriage.

On the western front, I am a sixth-generation Canadian, but it is my mother's background, that tangle of branches and roots planted so staunchly in English soil, which dominates this story.

~~~

She came from the protected world of the English upper class, from one of those snobbish family homes with an army of servants.

As a young woman she wanted out, wanted more than anything to get away from that world, but she could never have dreamed the future that unfolded for her.

And it is only when I delve into her past that I begin to understand the distance she has travelled from English gentry to a "classless" Canadian society; from being coddled by a cocoon of servants to having to do everything by and for herself. Yet there is more to Elizabeth than her well-heeled background. There is something different, something extraordinary about her makeup, something that I too may contain in my genes. So when I sit down to interview my mother, I am ostensibly asking about her past, but I am also self-consciously searching for another, less identifiable quality of character.

I am hoping, by examining my parents' journey, to find my own way home.

⚬

"I must have been incredibly naïve at 21," Elizabeth starts. "About the equivalent of a 14-year-old girl in Canada, probably. I think I never really considered the possible problems of moving halfway around the world."

We have not begun at the beginning, but I allow her this liberty.

"We'd originally planned that Eric would stay in England after the war, but when he was sent home, I was just anxious to rejoin him in Vancouver."

With no idea where she was headed, no knowledge of the in-laws or the country or even the lack of culture she'd find there, Elizabeth turned away from her native land without a thought. It seems an extreme reaction, moving halfway round the globe to escape family, but the question that piques me most is, who would I be if she'd stayed in England? In my mind I see English school children in their knee socks and blazers, and I wonder: would I have been a better Englishwoman than a Canadian?

I step back, try to imagine the transatlantic voyage that took her away from the known world of her youth, picturing the converted troop ship, its decks crowded with war brides waving goodbye.

And my mother, having no one to wave to — did she concentrate on the invisible shoreline ahead instead of the one receding behind her? Or was she wondering, watching the diminishing strip of green on the horizon, whether she might never see it again? On a cold day in February 1945, Elizabeth was heading somewhere it would not be easy to return from, certainly not affordable for many years. I consider how it must have felt to abandon everything familiar, and the desperation of that long-ago leave-taking makes my eyes water. Already.

Elizabeth continues talking, but I drift away as her facial expression blurs in front of me. I focus on her wool suit, cameo brooch on the lapel and pearl necklace at her neck, and force myself to come back to her voice. I need to understand more about the girl who made the rash decision to marry a colonial, go so far from home.

I ask her what I ask every immigrant.

"Where's home, Mom — here or there?"

And she doesn't hesitate, despite some harsh early years in Toronto with small babies and no friends, not even relatives to talk to while her husband hid behind mounds of law books.

"Canada, definitely," she declares.

How is it possible, I wonder, to live your youth in one country and call another land home?

"When I come home, I'm always glad to be back," my mother is saying.

I picture my mother inside a jet, stray whiffs of cloud drifting across the wing as the plane drops through the sky, and I remember the English patchwork of green and brown fields as seen from above. But when I look up and catch her eyes, I realize my mistake. She is speaking of Canada, not England.

Over Iceland, over Greenland, sometimes stopping to refuel in Newfoundland, Elizabeth has spent the last four decades crossing the North Pole at least once a year, going home to England, home to Canada. She's as much at home in a thick, Scandinavian sweater, face lit by the blaze of a campfire at my father's lakeside Cariboo hideaway, as she is in an English drawing room, drinking tea from a delicate Spode cup.

And her confident declaration of home only serves to underline my own confusion. Why am I not as clear as she whether the rugged peaks of B.C.'s Coastal Range or the worn green hills of west England are where I belong?

Elizabeth may not understand my struggle, but as a mother she has a strong desire to help. Sometimes now, when she is rummaging through her drawers in an effort to tidy up, she finds something that reminds her of my quest. Today she unearths a book from beneath a tangle of ribbon, stationery and wrapping paper in her desk, and she holds it out to me with a shy tentativeness.

"Perhaps this will be of interest to you?" she asks, unsure of what, exactly, I'm after.

It is a thin notebook from her secretarial days, a compilation of correspondence etiquette. I flip through it half-heartedly, not wanting to disappoint her, but sure it is nothing applicable to this story. I stop at a page of salutations, fresh evidence of the foreign world she's described so often.

"To the Queen," I read out loud, "a formal letter begins with *May it please your Majesty*, but a social letter begins with *Madam*. The envelope should read *To the Queen's most excellent Majesty* for formal purposes, and *To her Majesty the Queen* for social purposes." I laugh at the old-fashioned dictum, shake my head disapprovingly, a devout non-monarchist. Elizabeth is dismayed, chagrined by my blatant disrespect.

"But Mom," I protest when I notice her face. "When does anyone write a *social* letter to the Queen!"

She lifts her head just slightly, stands a bit taller, not amused. "The Queen has friends too, you know!"

"But really — do her friends have to call her '*Your Majesty?*' I mean, it's so pompous, for heaven's sake!"

"Well, she *is* the Queen, after all."

I stare at the evident disgust on her face and look away, avoiding contention by concentrating on the rest of the notebook. The pages open at sketches of insignia for the different military ranks, and once again I stop, interested, but also amazed by this radically different education from my own. Moments like these leave me feeling suspended between two worlds. Though I am born and raised a Canadian, and despite my search for a strong North American ancestor to ease the overseas draw, I feel closer to my English relatives. At the same time, however, there is an unfamiliar set of rules in my mother's past, the rudiments of which are so foreign to me that complete acceptance of my English background seems impossible. The world Elizabeth came from was constructed around an innate sense of what's done or not done; an inherent appreciation of life which was — perhaps still is — governed by seemingly arbitrary and ancient codes of behaviour. But many of these rules, like the etiquette regarding social dealings with the Queen, are utterly incomprehensible, even ridiculously false, to a middle-class North American.

I remember, during a dinner at my English grandmother's house, being sent to the pantry for a wine glass. I stood before the wall of glass-fronted cupboards, overwhelmed by the number and pieces of crystal stemware. Eventually, aware that the others were waiting, I selected a middling-sized wine glass, carried it back through the narrow hallways and presented it hopefully to my grandmother. The quiet seconds after I put the glass on the table were filled quickly by the realization that something was wrong. Later, I overheard my grandmother quizzing my mother about the kind of education my sister and I were receiving in Canada.

"But she doesn't know the difference between a claret and sauterne glass, my dear." From the landing above the drawing room, I could hear the frown in Anthea's voice.

Sometimes, despite my dual homing instincts, the chasm between these two worlds feels too large to bridge.

Young Lessons

*M*y mother was fed, entertained and contained in the nursery of Coates Manor, an ancient Gloucestershire seat whose name can be found in the Domesday Book. It was a conservative country house in which the traditional rule of thumb regarding children — that they should be seen and not heard — was upheld, though in Elizabeth's case the rule was more like neither seen nor heard.

Elizabeth, rebelling against her upbringing as stuffy and old-fashioned, raised my siblings and me by oscillating between the two extremes of free reign and strict discipline. In contrast to our mother's childhood, my brothers, sister and I careened through hallways and gardens, scattering toys and yells. We thundered across adult boundaries, totally unaware of the existence of grown-up sanctuaries. And depending on Elizabeth's ability to cope at any given moment, we were either indulged or reprimanded.

Stories from my continuum of memories alternately please or embarrass my mother, depending on their content. She smiles softly as I recall the drizzly school day when she surprised my sister and me with a bowl of anxious goldfish during a lunch of homemade french fries. But she frowns at my memory of the winter afternoon when I fell on glitzy, plastic dress-up shoes during my brother's birthday party, and she, annoyed, had to take me to the doctor to remove a metal buckle digging into my kneecap.

My sister and I often sat in the middle of a floor littered with the toys my mother never had, romanticizing stories from that long-ago childhood in front of an English nursery hearth. We dreamed of growing up and going back, returning to the protective cocoon of servants on a large estate, playing out our 1950s fantasy of marrying well, living happily ever after and being surrounded by leisure, money, irresponsibility. So far removed from that peaceful Gloucestershire manor, Elizabeth's stories served to camouflage our ordinary Canadian life so that only now can I appreciate the reality of what she survived during the transition to her new home.

Finding a place for herself in the more or less classless society of post-war Vancouver, struggling to be a parent in a world that revered children as much as the Brits ignored them, Elizabeth had to ad lib her way through those early years in Canada. Like most North American mothers in the 1950s, she performed as gardener, cook, chauffeur and maid — an enormous challenge for someone who'd never had to do any housework while growing up. In the wilds of the Canadian west and without any prior experience at running a household, Elizabeth learned the hard way, experimenting and making mistakes as she went along. She gave us what she knew, though some of it was too old-world to be of any use except, possibly, to confuse.

She taught my sister and me to sew, showing us the dainty embroidery stitches and careful running stitches of a household seamstress, sitting beside us like her own granny had beside her, demonstrating, watching, encouraging. And smiling, proud, when I brought home a gold-on-brown embossed badge, the Brownie award for achievement at needlework.

I try to imagine my mother as a child, seated next to her staunchly Victorian grandmother, matriarch of the clan. But that vision fades and is replaced by the faces of my old-world grandmother and great-aunt, the two members of English family so important in my Canadian upbringing. Granny Payne, the woman who was my namesake, and Great-Aunt Molly are the ones who told me about the others, those people whose faces are caught in family photographs but whose characters are only stories for me.

"Can we go over your mother's homes?" I ask my mother. Elizabeth takes a deep breath and then, counting on her fingers, lists the three homes prior to Coates Manor, the final family seat.

"Whirlow House," she explains, "is near Sheffield, the house where Anthea — Mother — was born. The house where BAF and MLF lived when they were first married." Elizabeth uses the initials inscribed on all the silver and books — everything inherited from Mary Lewton and Bernard Alexander Firth, her grandparents — the way the rest of us do, as family code for our ancestors.

"They moved to the large Sheffield estate, Norton Hall, while the children were still small," she continues. "And then they went to Clifton Maubank in Dorset. That was the house near Yeovil in Somerset, where I was born. The spooky old house," she reminds me. "The one Aunt Molly loved to tell ghost stories about."

My memory flits back to an English summer as I remember ...

"Clifton Maubank," my great-aunt Molly begins, "was the old, old house that —"

"Oh *don't* tell them those stories again!" Molly's sister, Anthea — my grandmother — rolls her eyes. "Really!" (*"Rally!"*)

"My dear Anthea," Molly returns, eyebrows raised in mock surprise, "they *want* to hear the stories again. Don't you, girls?" She looks at my sister and me. And the large grey eyes of little sister Bizzy — a nickname that stuck after my first attempt at "Elizabeth" came out as "Bizbuz" — grow as dark as the ravine back home, while I, at 10 or 11, scoff at her fear.

Molly begins again, starting with the story of the old woman whose face looked out the small attic window above the gables at Clifton Maubank. The sad visage gazed tiredly from beneath a bonnet of yellowed lace, but by the time someone else came to look, the woman had disappeared.

Bizzy, eyes widening dangerously, turns to look at my mother. She reaches out a hand for reassurance, then faces Molly again.

"Then there was the horse and carriage that could be heard for several minutes, coming up the long gravel drive, clop clop!" Molly's ringed hands dance in the air, imitating the prancing hooves. "But when the servants were sent to see who it was, there was nobody there!" Molly shakes her head to underline the inexplicable, then adds in a whisper, "It happened at least once a week."

And Bizzy slides back toward my mother's chair, presses against Elizabeth's stockinged legs.

"Were there any other ghosts?" I urge.

"Oh heavens, yes! There was an old monk in brown robes who used to wander through the gardens at unusual times, early mornings in the mist or mid-afternoons at teatime. And there was a white hare which somehow materialized inside the house, but by the time a gun was fetched, it had shot out the door into the garden and could not be found anywhere. Just when we'd set our minds on rabbit stew!"

Molly's eyes gleam, delighted with her dark powers.

"Tell us the other one, Aunt Molly," I beg. "The one about the chairs!"

Molly winks conspiratorially, and we move close to the small fire, shivering in spite of its heat. We ignore Anthea's disgusted sigh behind us.

"You mean the dining room at Clifton Maubank? Well, it was a large, fire-placed room with banks of small-paned windows overlooking the gardens. Every night at 7:00 we'd dress for dinner, meet at table for 7:30. Usually the fire would be lit and the curtains were open so that we could look out at the terrace. Then we'd start with our soup and get through that and some sort of fish. By the time we'd finished those first two courses, usually after the fish but sometimes at the beginning of the entrée, precisely at eight o'clock, we'd feel a strange tugging at our chairs. And whether we liked it or not, the chairs would all be pulled back from the table, occupied or empty!"

"Every night, Aunt Molly?" I squeak, delighted.

"Yes, my dear, *every* night."

From the corner of my eye I see my sister crawling onto my mother's lap, the smoke from Anthea's Egyptian cigarette curling above her tight waves of grey hair while one knee bounces impatiently over the other.

"Weren't you scared?" I ask.

Molly waves the question away, tossing her head lightly. "Oh, *lots* of old English houses have funny things going on in them. You get used to it," she shrugs. Leaning close then, Molly brings her brown eyes nearer and lowers her voice.

"But the music room — *that* was the worst room of all!" I hug my knees closer to my chest. "It was separate from the main house. We used it as a playroom, going there in the evenings with our brothers and friends. And outside the doors of the music room, the dogs — who came with us everywhere — would balk, flatten their ears and turn around to go back. We had to drag them in, make them come with us for the evening, and they'd spend the whole time whimpering and cowering at the door, their hackles raised!" Molly's voice rises majestically on the last phrase and she sits back, eyes glowing.

Anthea harrumphs impatiently and Elizabeth hugs Bizzy a little tighter.

"Why, Aunt Molly?" my sister whimpers into the silence.

"Ghosts, child! *Ghosts!* Dogs are *terribly* sensitive to the other side, you know."

"Molly, really! (*rally!*)" My grandmother stands with extreme displeasure, displacing Molly's spotlight.

We are sent off to bed then, Bizzy reluctant to mount the dark stairs, myself vaguely worried about the fact that all old English houses have ghosts. I tell our mother that we are very thirsty and ask her to leave the hall light on after saying good night.

Much later, after tense concentration on the rustling leaves and wind outside, I hear Bizzy cry out. I listen to the soothing tones of my mother's voice and the faint shuffle of slippers in the hallway and then the silence again. After a while, I raise the covers, let my feet slide across the tight linen sheets to the carpet, eyeing the black corner by the washstand as I sit up. I slip across the dark landing outside my door, a spectre in my long white nightgown, and into my mother's room. The old bed creaks as I squeeze myself between the edge and my sister, finding a place to fall asleep, reprieved.

～⌒～

When, years later, I find the 37-page prospectus *Clifton Maubank Estate, Dorset, For Sale By Auction, 1925,* I peer at the photographs in it. Page by page, I search the attic windows, look for the morose face of an old woman in a lacy bonnet. I search for a hare in the great hallways, the monk in the garden, but what I see is the set for a Hollywood remake of *Wuthering Heights*, a dark-windowed, eerily gaunt old house built in the flat façade of a bygone era. The auctioneers' offering describes the estate as a "stone-built Tudor Manor House, with a 14th Century Annexe" — the music room — "together with Home Farm, four dairies, Clifton Wood, and other accommodations on an estate of about 1,500 acres."

At the back of the prospectus is a pocket containing an inserted map. When I remove and unfold the map, coloured areas like those of a grade-school social studies project outline woods, the various farms, the River Yeo, the long road where the never-seen carriages were heard to approach, the railways to London and Weymouth. And despite my socialist disgust at the preposterous amount of land for one family, I find myself wishing we still owned an estate like Clifton Maubank.

The gardens in particular lure me. Descriptions of the lily pond, flagged Dutch gardens, sunken lawns, rose and flower gardens, an early Georgian gazebo, small yew bower, herb garden, three orchards and a walled kitchen garden — all fill me with longing. So much space in which to sit in solitude, feel removed from the rest of the world, wander noncommittally.

Those were better times. Unreal times.

When I turn back to the beginning of the prospectus to read the descriptions of the old house, though, I wince. Sixteen bedrooms in two separate wings; three bathrooms (English style, larger than a North American living room) and five reception rooms for entertaining, dining, dancing.

Who could ever need 16 bedrooms, I wonder. "It's pretentious," I say to Elizabeth. "A very pretentious lifestyle."

Going Back

*O*utside my parents' Vancouver home is a meandering golf course, its open green space dotted with the towering cedars and hemlocks of my native landscape. The greenness reaches through the window and into the cozy living room dominated by my grandmother's old furniture. Huge cabinets from the library of that other Anthea, displays of Royal Worcester and Crown Derby behind their glass-fronted doors, make the room feel tight, crowded. So many of the pieces are too delicate and invaluable to actually eat from, but Elizabeth loves the porcelain for its history and connection to her past. The teapots and cups stare loftily from behind the glass doors, and, beside the cabinets, heavy gilt-framed oils and watercolours of English landscapes and unnameable ancestors complete the shrine. The scene is one familiar to me: salal and salmonberry reflected in the polished surface of old mahogany; the incongruity of raw nature in the midst of civilized trappings.

Whenever my mother and father go to England, usually in the spring or fall, the problem of a house-sitter for all these valuable possessions arises. Several times it has happened that I have been between homes and able to fill that post for them. In 1995, when I have completed my research and am trying to find a way to put all the notes and interviews and documents together, the house-sitting situation comes available once more.

After kissing my mother on the cheek, I stand in the doorway as they leave. A puff of too much perfume is left behind as Elizabeth hurries down the front steps. "Goodbye, goodbye!" she calls from the other side of the suitcase trundling reluctantly behind her. Her free hand waves in the air, whether at my father waiting in the car or me, I can't tell. Her feet land in short, flat slaps, rocking her heaviness from side to side, a stilted gait that reminds me of my grandmother. I retreat inside the house and watch the rest of their departure through the window, waving once as the car pulls into the street and disappears round a curve. The annual pilgrimage to Gloucestershire has begun.

After their rushed departure, I find various bits of Eric and Elizabeth's morning routine scattered throughout the house. A cereal bowl with its remaining puddle of milk in the kitchen sink; the morning paper, neatly folded into removable sections at the foot of Elizabeth's bed; a half-finished mug of tea on Eric's bedside table. I reach for the mug and then the paper, sloshing tea as I bend over the sports page. The wetness creeps toward the edge of the paper, but I frown at the contents of the mug, realizing something for the first time. My father's tea is black.

Disconcerted — understanding that this milkless tea is somehow blasphemous in light of our strong British background — I gather the newspaper quickly and leave the room in a blur of confusion. As if it were a bowl of rotting fruit, I carry the evidence of Eric's defection well in front of me, moving through the dark hallway and jogging instinctively at the bulge of staircase as I hurry toward the sunlit kitchen in the distance, a rat taking the shortest route through the maze. At the sink, I deposit the mug beside the cereal bowl and stand back, look at the blackness of that tea again and realize the smallness of the detail. It's such an insignificant point, but something I feel I should have — must have — known before about this man, my father. The truth is, there are many things I don't know about him.

I focus on the mug in order to avoid the truth. It is one of Elizabeth's favourites, with a slogan on its side. "If it's not running right," the slogan says, "speak with the original owner." Above these words is a black-and-white photograph taken from space, Earth enveloped by clouds. The mug, one of a collection for which Elizabeth has assuredly paid too much, is marketed by the Anglican Church of Canada. Since none of the family, particularly her husband, will accompany her to Sunday church, she is reduced to using gimmicks like these mugs, offering us tea or coffee with a message when we visit.

I last went to church with Eric and Elizabeth several years ago on Christmas Eve. The holiday congregation was dotted with the faces of school friends' parents and, warmed by wine from dinner, I relaxed into the hug of familiar community. I stood beside my aging parents in a haze of contentment, joining them in song and reliving memories of some earlier Christmases. After the first two carols, though, Eric seemed to lag behind, his voice stopping and starting like a shorted-out loudspeaker. When I turned toward him, eyebrows lifted in wordless inquiry, Eric's confusion was visible. His blank eyes lifted from the hymnal to the candlelit altar, searching for the words he could neither read nor remember.

A growing tightness squeezed at my throat and I turned away, floundering through the next few lines. Moments later, hoping he'd found his place and caught us up, I stole another sideways glance. This time Eric's hand was on his brow, the red-haired knuckles of stubby fingers and a flash of gold signet ring wiping quickly over his eyes. My father never cries, never demonstrates much of a reaction for life except when he drinks more than usual, changing at those times from a stern, curt man into a facetiously soppy, bleary-eyed stranger. Hardened by years of those drunken performances, I told myself that this Christmas Eve show of emotion was only the result of another round of over-consumption.

Most of the truths I know are painful.

Anglican Church services incorporate a mixture of kneeling, standing and sitting. Twice during the rest of that Christmas service,

Eric was just completing the process of kneeling when the time came to stand again. I watched him struggle against the unwillingness of a stiffened leg and then, when the tension in my throat felt like the slash of a knife, I looked away. My eyes rose to the softly lit cross in front of us, and a sudden blast of humility jolted through my skull, threatening my eyes with hot tears. In the middle of "Silent Night," all attention swallowed by my heart, my vocal chords seized and I could only mouth the words of that favourite carol.

For the rest of the service, Eric remained seated, leaving an obvious gap in the wave of bodies that stood, heads bowing and lifting, to sing. His deep voice wafted up to meet mine whenever his sporadic memory fed him some words, and he tried to follow along in the prayer book but eventually gave up, adding only a commanding "Amen" at the end of the minister's intonations.

I felt a curious mixture of fierce protectiveness and embarrassment for my father that evening. Wanting simultaneously to hide and draw attention to the obviously incapacitated man beside me, I periodically shifted my weight to cover or emphasize the conspicuous hole in the standing congregation. At the same time, I scanned the nearby faces of other singers, daring them to throw a disapproving glance at the seated body beside mine.

Halfway through the final carol, it occurred to me that I had no real investment in the protocol of the Anglican Church; from my aloof position I was invulnerable to the opinions of the congregation. If there really is a God, I told myself, He does not frown on Eric's shortcomings. Why should I?

<hr />

The memory over, I tiptoe — a reaction to the fuss of my mother's panicked departure — out of the kitchen and down the hallway. I hesitate at the entrance to the living room full of lofty furnishings.

I am momentarily awed by my responsibility: these weighty possessions, this house and well-manicured garden, seem suddenly, overwhelmingly important. The stuff and things that will one day be divided between my brother and sister and me and thence our children

— a discussion we have so far been able to avoid — look at me haughtily, as if I'm incapable of managing such wealth. I am.

Turning, I see how the early-morning light washes over the dining room table and I decide to set up a work space there, placing myself so the flood of sunbeams will kiss the back of my neck as I sit at the computer. I put on a recording of *Madame Butterfly* while I unpack my computer and boxes of notes. Max, my mongrel Jack Russell, wanders disconsolately from room to room, her nails clacking softly up and down the hardwood, looking for a place to call home. She settles ultimately at my feet, tail over nose and eyes, a perfectly curled circle, ears flexing at the sound of Puccini in this house where usually there are only loud voices or silences — my parents growing old, growing deaf.

In the Beginning

*W*hen I first arrived with a tape recorder to interview my mother about her fading childhood memories, the formality of the situation seemed to prompt a resumption of her former accent. As if she were aware of the importance of the details I was about to ask her, as if going back to that tight elocution and concise enunciation would help to reincarnate a younger self, her voice turned again to the clipped cadence of the British. I felt myself begin to focus on the lilting, almost singsong sound rather than the phrases and descriptions she used, my freedom to wander assured by the whirring of the tape recorder in front of us. I closed my eyes, heard in her alternating pitch and oscillating emphasis more about what she was saying than her diction revealed.

I have lived with my mother's Oxford dialect long enough to discern the aural nuances of sarcasm, disgust, approval. There is a whole substrata of language in the Queen's English that belies a Briton's lack of facial expression. Now, listening to her voice on the tape recorder, I begin to realize that I am embarking on an exploration of more consequence than I initially imagined. The investigation of my dual heritage will be a journey of therapeutic proportions.

⌒

"How far back can you go?" the tape begins.

Elizabeth responds to my queries without apparent stops at the ends of sentences, as if she must hurry to get everything out before she forgets or before she is interrupted.

"I can really just remember sitting in the nursery at the manor trying to eat my meals. Bland, stodgy things like porridge. And rice pudding!" My mother screws up her face at that memory. "And if you didn't eat your lunch, it got dished up again at supper time. And there was a fireplace with those old blue and white Delft tiles and a screened fender 'round the front. Those high nursery fenders were meant to keep children from falling into the fire — hopefully — and we used to hang things to dry there too. There was a window facing toward the paddock at the back and the farmland beyond and there was another window that faced south, southeast over the dining room. And I remember two rather old family portraits in there, which were so bad that my grandmother had banned them to the nursery. I think she eventually got so annoyed that she had them put in the pond."

"In the pond?"

"In the pond. When she got tired of things she'd say, 'Here, child, you take this and dump it in the pond,' which I thought was great fun."

"What else do you remember dumping in the pond?

"Oh, old brass lamps that wobbled too much and just strange things every once in a while."

"Where was the pond?"

"On the right as you came up the main drive toward the front entrance of the house."

"Was it deep enough to swim in?"

"Probably. I'd never been allowed to swim in it, being from a non-swimming household."

"But obviously if you could sink brass lamps in it, it was."

"Oh, no — they were down at the bottom with all the sludge and slime and stuff and there were lovely newts which used to live there and I'd catch them in a butterfly net and keep them in a jam jar in my bedroom for a few days and they usually died, poor things."

There is a dreamy look on Elizabeth's face as she wanders through the hallways of her memories. But my mother has a tendency to digress, jumping without warning from the memory of an individual to some apparently unrelated incident. When I notice her in a quiet moment of recollection, then, I guide her gently back to her childhood.

"What else did you dump in the pond?"

She smiles. "Can't remember, but I expect if somebody dug it up, some archaeologist in the distant future, he'd have a lovely time."

"Who were the portraits of, do you know? The ones that Granny May banished to the nursery?"

"I think they were old Firth portraits — maybe the first Thomas Firth of the steel foundry."

"Your great-grandfather?"

"Yes. Anyway, they were just sort of dreary portraits of an old man with a beard on a black background. Not a very interesting face one way or another; they certainly weren't a great loss to the nation."

"It wasn't that she didn't like the man in the portrait, then —"

"No, no. She just thought they were crummy pictures that weren't worth hanging in the hall." Elizabeth considers something, then adds, "I hope she kept the frames; they were rather nice ones ..." She stares at something I can't see, remembering again.

I jump in quickly before she slips into thoughts of other pictures, other walls. "So what else do you remember about your nursery?"

Her grey eyes turn to me, staring blankly, then refocus slowly on my questioning face.

"The nursery?" she repeats. "Well, there was a big table in the centre. And an armchair." Another pause. "And I really remember old Frithy — who was Miss Frith, Granny's housekeeper — who sat there and sewed and sewed and sewed. She was either sewing curtains or bedspreads or putting name tapes on towels, sheets, blankets or something. In a big household in those days there was always something to be sewn, day in, day out, you know."

"Was she your nanny as well?"

"No. She was my grandmother's lady's maid. But she was also in charge of all the little underlings in the house, who, I think, lived in great fear of her. I thought she was a sweet old lady. To me she was old because she had white hair, but I think she'd always had white hair, for some funny reason, and it was done up sort of *bouffant* —"

Elizabeth's exaggerated French accent snaps my eyes away from the notepad in my lap, from the thoughts I scribble as she speaks, but she continues without me "— Edwardian style, and she always wore a long skirt right to the ground, and her keys for various cupboards and secret places all hanging on a chain off her waistband. Quite sort of Victorian looking."

"Stockings?"

"Oh yes, *dear* yes!

"High collars?"

"Yes, oh yes. She really was quite of *that* era, you know."

We both pause, imagining Frithy in front of us, each with our own image of that long-ago time.

"How old do you think Frithy was really?"

"Oh, she was probably younger than I am now. Fifty or 60, perhaps. She had been with my grandmother for many, many years, coming down from Yorkshire with the family like all the rest of the retainers."

Granny May, as Elizabeth knew her grandmother, was the undeniable head of the family until her death. For me, though, meeting this matriarchal great-grandmother through my mother's stories, Mary Lewton Firth is much more than head of the clan. Despite having many times unscrolled the handwritten family tree tracing my ancestors back to the time of William the Conqueror, I think of Mary Lewton Firth as the beginning of my English history, a kind of source point.

Raised by a maternal aunt after her mother died in childbirth, Mary had very little contact with her father. Edward Lewton Penne joined the Royal Navy as a chaplain after his wife's death, staying in touch with his daughter only through the mail. Edward regularly sent home small, leather-bound volumes of watercolour images painted during his ship's stops in colonial ports. On my bedroom wall is a grouping of his African scenes from the 1880s: minute donkeys leaning into a steep trail winding up the hot, yellow rock of a Tenerife cliff. Beside the donkeys, a Zanzibar woman, white eyes in a dark face staring from beneath a large headdress of small barrels.

In 1887, at age 20, Great-Grandmother Mary Lewton Penne married Bernard Alexander Firth, fourth son of Sheffield businessman Mark Firth. According to a small volume entitled *The History of the Firth's* [sic] (Thos. Firth & Sons, Ltd., Sheffield, 1924), Mark Firth ranks "in the history of Sheffield as the most outstanding man of the 19th century." He was not, the biographer states, "born with a silver spoon in his mouth, but was the son of parents of the mechanic class ..." From this one small comment I understand that the Firth family wealth is directly traceable to Elizabeth's great-grandfather's enterprising nature during the Industrial Revolution. In other words, my mother's family was part of the (distasteful, to Elizabeth's mind) "nouveau riche." It is a small point to some, but one that looms unforgivingly in the shadows of my mother's memories.

In the heyday of those early Sheffield steel foundries, Thos. Firth & Sons was raised "to the greatest heights as [steel] manufacturers" and Mark's new wealth enabled him to donate almshouses and parks, and even found a college in the city. Perhaps because he was "very much interested in the ... well-being and welfare of the Sheffield people," Mark was elected to the post of Master Cutler for the three succeeding years from 1867 to '69 and then, in 1874, he was elected mayor of Sheffield.

Mark raised his sons in anticipation of the fine future he'd begun for them. Bernard, Mary Lewton's future husband, and his brothers were schooled at Rugby and introduced early on to "good" society, including royalty. In August 1875, the Firths' 26.5-acre estate at Oakbrook hosted the Prince and Princess of Wales, Albert Edward and Alexandra, during an official visit to Sheffield. It was this event, I now think, that has so often been dredged up as proof of my English family's stature. Somehow that distant connection to royalty meant that we were "above" most Canadians, though now the story seems more of a legend, even a source of embarrassment, than something to boast about.

It was probably Mary's more than Bernard's family background that elevated my ancestors' status. As Elizabeth says, Mary Lewton's family came from "landed gentry of away back."

"And yet," Elizabeth's eyes widen conspiratorially, "Mary was kind of a naughty girl." When I ask what that means, she tells me Mary's behaviour was frequently not fitting for a woman of her class.

Mary Lewton would often, for instance, enjoy a cigarette with coffee after the evening meal. In the 1920s, when the rigid rules of society were being challenged, many young women began to smoke, and "everyone" kept a cigarette box on their table. "When somebody came to visit, you offered them a cigarette the second they sat down. Most young people smoked, but for a lady of 60-plus, like Granny May, that was quite something."

It was precisely this "gay Edwardian" attitude that attracted the young Bernard Firth. He was, apparently, so smitten with Mary that "he just tolerated what she wanted; anything she asked for she got."

It is Mary who kept the details of their luxurious lifestyle, recording the specifics for occasions when she and Bernard entertained friends and VIPs, initially at Whirlow House, their "small" first home of some 15 bedrooms, and then at Norton Hall, the massive estate the family moved to in the early 1900s. One of my favourite archives is a red, leather-bound book embossed on the cover with gold lettering: *Home Dinners.* This was Mary's diary of the various menus, guests and occasions hosted in their earlier years.

On the left-hand pages of *Home Dinners* are copies of menu cards from each event, and on the right-hand page, specific details: the time and date, a sketch of the seating plan, the flower arrangements at table and in the library (where coffee and brandy were served after the meal), the name of the china and crystal service used and the name of the cook preparing the dinner. For a number of occasions, a printed invitation and program embossed with the Firth coat of arms are attached. The ostentation is pretentious to me, a child of middle-class experience, but alluring nevertheless.

Some of the gatherings mentioned in *Home Dinners* catered to book societies, horse-racing fans, cricket parties or the staff at Norfolk Works steel mill. And it is noteworthy to me that the parties Mary logs as "ordinary" often comprised as many as 14 guests, most with titles: Captain Galway, Sir Alex Wilson, Lord Hawke, etc. But even at these "ordinary" meals, the menus were lavish and extreme. On February 12, 1904, for a small, at-home luncheon, Mary Lewton's menu reads: *Fresh Oysters, Turbot with lobster sauce, Fried Sole, Kidneys à la Berlin, Monaco Timbales, Saddle of Mutton, Boiled Chickens, Grouse Pistachio Bavaroise, Meringues, Herring Roe, Luxette Croutes, Ices.*

For January 14, 1909, the invitation reads:

> *Mr. Bernard A. Firth*
> *at Home*
> *at the Cutlers' Hall*
> *Thursday January 14th 1909*
> *Dancing*   *R.S.V.P.*
> *9 to 1:30*   *Norton Hall*

On this occasion, Mary records 277 guests at dining tables graced with pink carnations and arrangements of white tulips, lily-of-the-valley and hyacinths in the huge drawing room. A copy of the dance card lists the program of music for eight dances before and ten after supper. Twelve valses, several two-steps, two lancers and one polka brought the guests to a final valse, the "Eton Boat Song," followed by a galop to "John Peel." (Apparently "John Peel" was a traditional favourite: the dance programs from December 28, 1905, through to July 17, 1914, all finished with the same galop.) I picture the silk gowns and glittering diamonds on the women, the tails and waistcoats on the men, and I sense how far removed my life is from that world. I would have felt more at ease as one of the maids attending the guests, a presence moving unnoticed through the gathering.

The one entry in the red book that seems somehow remiss is the King and Queen's July 12, 1905, visit to Sheffield. Mary Lewton must have been too engaged with overseeing her staff to keep notes for the occasion, because the entry for that particular evening reflects only that King of Denmark geraniums were used as table decorations and the guests included "Two generals, etc., etc."

But my favourite entries — the ones where my imagination runs amok with visions of broad-brimmed hats and long, lacy gowns, gloves and dainty leather button boots — are the garden parties:

Mrs. Bernard Firth
at Home
Thursday July 30th, 1903
3:30 to 6:30
Norton Hall
nr. Sheffield   R.S.V.P.

On this occasion there is a band, the 1st Hallamshire Volunteer Battalion of the Yorkshire and Lancaster Regiment. Bandmaster J. Tait entertained guests with a two-part repertoire including Drescher's "La Ritirata Italiana," Karker's "The Belle of New York," Schubert's then-popular "Standchen," a selection from Bizet's *Carmen*, the Meissler valse "In Old Madrid," Thorne's "Simple Amen" and the Spanish serenade of "La Paloma." Ladies with parasols strolled the grounds, nodding fashionably hatted heads in quiet acknowledgment of a familiar face across the lawn and sipping gracefully from glasses of champagne or claret. At tables heavy with platters, delicately gloved hands aimed sterling tines at an opulence of nectarines, peaches, strawberries, melons, plums, pineapples. Tittering laughter hovered above the grounds as guests leaned to choose from sandwiches of lobster, foie gras, potted chicken, potted meat or cress and anchovy. Later, as tea and coffee were served in the finest bone china, the afternoon idled away to the music drifting through the air.

From the distance of the 21st century, it's a scene right out of the movies, or a description from a Victorian novel, replete with fantasy.

Exodic Memories

*M*ary's enormous entertainment budget was due in part to Bernard's business involvements. Like his father before him, Bernard was Master Cutler of Sheffield, an "expensive honour bestowed on a business leader of the community" and one that necessitated the frequent and lavish entertaining of other businessmen and their families. When he became the director of two railway lines, Bernard found himself more often away from home on business, leaving Mary to manage the household finances. Elizabeth tells me that Bernard allowed Mary to spend freely because he "worshipped the ground she walked on. I guess he did anything to placate and keep her quiet so he could get on with his business and do whatever he had to do."

But though my mother remembers her grandmother with fondness, she remembers very little about her grandfather. "He was up in Sheffield or in London nearly all the time. He only came down [to Gloucestershire] for brief weekends and half that time he was either out shooting or hunting the hounds." And when Bernard was in residence at Coates Manor, Elizabeth was still so young that she spent most of her day in the nursery, removed from the adult world. "I only appeared at meals on rare occasions, maybe Sunday lunch or something." Nonetheless, in the seven years that Elizabeth knew her grandfather, Bernard left a warm impression on her.

"Do you remember him?" I ask her now.

"Just. He was rather nice," Elizabeth's voice underlines "nice" and her face softens as she recalls her grandfather, the only male relative seen regularly in childhood, "and it was always rather special when he was just there, sometimes, on a Sunday. He had pale blue eyes and rather an aristocratic-looking face. A very good-looking man, quiet and self-effacing. Do you want to go back to the nursery?"

I am startled out of dreamy imaginings about my great-grandfather, and for a moment I stare at her uncomprehendingly. It is suddenly pointless to try and unearth Bernard as a personality; it was the 1920s when Elizabeth knew him, and adults weren't assessed by children. They just *were*.

"Wherever your head goes," I say. And I wonder, as soon as I've said it, whether I've been unwise.

"So then other than the nursery," Elizabeth begins, "there was the linen room next door which was twice as big again, full of huge cupboards with sheets and towels and goodness-knows-what and my rocking horse stood right in the middle of this rather large, bare room where I think the ironing used to be done. So I could play on it ..."

"While they ironed?"

"Oh, I don't think there was ever anybody there with me. I don't remember."

"Why wasn't your rocking horse in the nursery?"

"There wouldn't have been room, I guess, or it wouldn't have been convenient. It wasn't really a nursery, you see, it was just a room that we sat in. I don't ever remember playing with toys."

The comment stabs at me, brings me back to the present. Sometimes Elizabeth tells me things that make me cringe with remorse for the small, only child raised by such distant adults. Nannies and relatives who had no empathy for children and their games, no idea, perhaps no memories, of their own childhood. I imagine the young Elizabeth, her short body and dark bobbed hair towered over by ceiling-high cupboards of bleached white linens — sheets, towels, tablecloths, dinner napkins — starched, ironed and folded to perfection. And a small child, rocking, rocking.

"But your bed was in the nursery?" I protest 70 years later.

"No, no. That was another room again. There were —" Elizabeth pauses, counting on her fingers. "One … two … three … four … five … six or more maids' bedrooms in the back wing of the manor, and I had one of those rooms with my nanny. My nanny had reddish hair, sort of fading to grey, and this grey herringbone tweed skirt and jacket and a white blouse up to her neck. And I remember sharing a room with her and being told to turn my face to the wall while she put on all her corsets and marvellous garments in the early morning, so I don't think she bent over very much. I think she was quite kind but rather severe and a bit strict. She certainly wasn't the kind of person you could have any affection for. And after she left, a friend of mother's called Bennie Lubbock — whose mother was old Lady Lubbock?"

Elizabeth looks at me with raised eyebrows, waiting for me to recognize the name. When I shake my head dumbly, she expands: "Her father was the astronomer Herschel? Who discovered some planet — I forget which one, Herschel's planet or something." I shrug at her, admitting my ignorance although the name Herschel does ring a bell, and she continues. "Anyway, Bennie was a single woman and she was sweet and fun and a nice friend. She didn't seem like a nanny. I guess she came more like a sort of governess, an in-between kind of person."

"Was she young?"

"Well, my mother was young then so I should think she was. I suppose they were about thirtyish at the most."

It's strange to hear my mother admit that her mother was young once. Elizabeth has always maintained that her mother worked at being old, as though that were Anthea's biggest fault. Curious to me to hear a daughter speak so harshly about her mother, but then the circumstances were much different for Elizabeth than they have been for me.

One day I find a box of old home movies, so I set up the projector, urge Elizabeth to come watch with me. On one canister of film someone has written "APP & APEB," my grandmother's and my own initials.

We sit on opposite ends of the living-room couch as the 8-mm film flickers and jumps through scratched frames, watching a small child dressed in jodhpurs and jacket toddling back and forth on the screen and squinting in the sunlight.

"That's you, you know." Elizabeth raises her eyebrows at me. I look closer at the white-blonde curls, the wrinkled nose and determined look, but I don't recognize the child. I can't feel how it was in that small body.

"I bought that suit in London," she says. "It was very expensive — yellow corduroy from Harrod's. I wanted you to look nice for your granny. I waited until the last leg of the train trip before I put you in it, but somehow you managed to crawl under the carriage seats and get covered in grease and soot anyway." She shakes her head, remembering the dismay as if it were today's latest disappointment.

Perhaps it was that first trip — as well as the later travels up the B.C. coast, into the Canadian heartland, over the choppy Atlantic, into strange and exotic lands — that gave me, at a young age, a feeling of rootlessness. On this filmed trip I am being presented: the first granddaughter brought back to the English west country, my other roots. Behind the unfamiliar child on the screen I see a patchwork of gold and green fields stretching toward the rolling Cotswold hills. On the other side, bordering the lawn beyond the tottering infant, is a stand of giant beech and elm trees planted in the time of Prince Albert.

Granny Payne, the woman who is my namesake, dressed in tweed skirt and oxfords, is already stiff with age in this 1952 film. I do a quick mental calculation: the celluloid me on the screen is not yet a year old. How old is this other, the original, Anthea? I think of the blue-enamelled locket in the shape of a heart, lying forgotten in a dark jewellery box, commemorating the year of my grandmother's birth. Two nines outlined in diamond chips — 1899. In this fuzzy picture, then, Granny Payne is 53, though she looks much older.

Despite a privileged upbringing, Anthea was a very melancholic soul, worrying incessantly about finances, the future, life. It must have been the unseen weight of those worries that bowed her shoulders, already stooping and tired on the movie screen before me.

I search her face, dark-circled eyes and full lips, looking for something that says she was young once. When she bends to retrieve a ball, rolling it across the lawn toward me, the stiffness of that movement reaches off the screen like a withered hand brushing my face. Decades after this moment was filmed, I remember walking with my grandmother, slowing to accommodate her peculiarly rocking gait, old hips and knees seized with the pain of arthritis that plagued her 'til the end.

On the screen, yellow corduroy jodhpurs run toward the ball, slipping below the camera lens when the short legs stumble. The baby face toys with a pout before rolling over, leaning forward on chubby fists and pushing up. Ball reached, it no longer attracts, and now a pudgy hand points at the sky, a round "Oh!" on baby lips. Granny Payne smiles indulgently, holds out a small bonnet and rocks forward to place it on my head. I run away. The game continues for another minute of film, the hat is pushed on in a moment of distraction, but two fat little hands rip it off again and the adults laugh.

Look at the camera, Annie! Look at Mummy! Anthea's fleshy lips move as her finger points at the audience. When finally my face turns, the eyes disappear, blue irises swallowed by wrinkles of fat as I squint into the sunlight.

This squint is the only thing I recognize about the child on the screen. Pictures of me at different ages, eyes screwed up tight at the glare of ordinary daylight, fill pages of family photograph albums. When I grew old enough to recognize the unattractiveness of my squint, I refused to pose for any more photos.

"Granny hated having her picture taken," Elizabeth interrupts my thoughts. "Just like you."

A suggestion of nostalgia in her voice, like a dart of sunlight between briefly shifting clouds, surprises me. But Elizabeth, so far away at the other end of the couch, has pulled back into herself when I turn to look, her face dark and brooding. My mother carries a sizeable amount of regret for her own mother, a woman for whom she felt more fear than love. I turn back to the film, leave the subject untouched because of my own lost ache for the grandmother I still miss.

Family Practice

*W*hen I ask Elizabeth to remember her aunt and uncles for me, her memory flits unconnectedly.

Mary Lewton and Bernard Alexander Firth had five children. Alexander Mark Bernard, known as Alec, was almost five years older than the next in line and, after childhood, didn't have much to do with his siblings.

"I remember that once, when I was little, he kicked Bobby, the dog, and I disliked him from then on." With that, The Eldest Son is dismissed.

Bernard and Mary's other four children were close. Mark Montague and Kathleen Mary (Molly), third and fourth respectively, were only a year apart in age and spent an inseparable childhood on the rambling acreage at Norton Hall, an estate that included its own church, extensive farmlands and a private lake. Charles Phillimore Lewton (Phil), the second eldest, made it his job to look after Baby Anthea, who eventually grew up to be very dependent on her elder brother.

While still children, of the age when Bernard and Mary would not have spent much time with them, all five little Firths had a nanny, various governesses and several tutors, whose ultimate job was to instill good manners.

"That," insists Elizabeth, "made life a hell of a lot easier for parents in those days."

Alec was sent to Rugby, but Mark and Phil, who both developed asthma, had a permanent tutor during their younger years. Eventually the two boys went to Malvern College in the healthy air of the Malvern Hills, and the tutor was kept on to do general accounts for the Firth household. Uncle John, as the tutor became known, was the sickly cousin of "some poor relative who managed to persuade Bernard or May to give him a home and living." John remained on Granny May's household staff, in spite of her children's thinly disguised hatred of him, until her death and the subsequent sale of her estate.

With her second son, Phil, Mary Lewton had a special connection. "She woke up suddenly one night in the middle of the war and it turned out later on that was the exact time Phil was wounded." Elizabeth raises her eyebrows at me and explains, "He got himself all shot up in his *private parts* during the First World War." Without asking, I assume this to be the reason for his childlessness.

"Mark," she continues, "moved with a pretty free-living, jet-set crowd in the 1920s. A lot of gin and champagne, and his wife, Aunt Helen, was a little *fast*, as they would say."

"Fast?"

"I can remember she once got hauled up on the mat in front of Granny and she was being lectured on having gone off on a yacht with another man. Probably I shouldn't have heard, but I was eavesdropping. And Granny made it clear she wasn't going to have any of *that* sort of nonsense in her family, you see."

"Was Helen suitably chastised or did she talk back?"

Elizabeth chokes on her laughter. "Granny was a *real* dictator, rather like Queen Victoria. I mean, you *didn't* talk back to her. I presume Helen was shaken up by the scolding or at least clever enough to *act* as if she was."

"Was that why Uncle Mark was round and portly and red-faced?" I ask. "Because of his lifestyle?"

"Mark and Helen gambled a lot on the races and lost pots of money trying to live beyond their means. Drinking champagne every day with people like the Rothschilds, going to the most expensive clubs and the most expensive hotels — it doesn't last forever." Elizabeth recalls how Mark once boasted to my father, a man totally unfamiliar with the kind of wealth common to the Firths' social class, that "nobody with any sense has a bank account in the black. I've lived in the red for years quite successfully."

Mark, like brother Alec, was eased out of the family business when he showed neither interest nor acumen. With the lump sum from his golden handshake, Mark bought a huge estate on the Scottish coast. Knockbrex was intended to — and did — open doors of introduction to the rich shooting crowd in Scotland. "He was very keen on shooting," Elizabeth assures me, as though the keenness should excuse his extravagance.

I am very keen on being rich myself, I muse, wondering for perhaps the Nth time why I was born to this generation and not the other Anthea's.

Anthea and Molly were educated differently than their brothers. When Molly, older by two years, went to school in London, Anthea remained at home alone, squirrelled away behind the high stone walls of the estate with no other young people to talk to during the long days. Having only her mother for a companion, Anthea must have watched Mary with the growing assumption that one day she would have to perform in the same capacity. But Mary Lewton's grand role as hostess and matriarch was too much for the timid Anthea, and so, very early on, she retreated into the role of the invalid.

While still very young, Anthea had contracted measles and pneumonia simultaneously, a situation that tainted the rest of her life. In those days, such a medical complication usually proved fatal, so the family had prepared itself for the baby's death. When Anthea survived, her convalescence and subsequent childhood illnesses were monitored so fastidiously that a gradual acceptance of her extreme fragility seems an understandable consequence. From that time, Anthea's delicate health was reflected in her nickname: she was still called "Baby" by Frithy, the manor housekeeper, when Elizabeth was herself a young girl of ten or more.

So when all her siblings were sent off to boarding schools, Anthea was schooled at home by various governesses, all of whom she hated.

Eventually she was sent to join Molly at the Brondesbury Institution for Young Ladies in London, but Anthea was apparently "unsuited" for such a move. Something "went wrong" and she was brought home at the end of her first term.

Elizabeth raises her eyebrows when she presents this latter bit of information and then adds, in a suggestively delicate voice, "She didn't *like* it so she went back home again …"

"Was she just too timid a child, then?"

"One *term*, not one year. One *term*."

"And just saying she didn't like it would have been enough to bring her home?"

"She was very shy, a very shy person. All her life she was awfully reserved and had no idea how to make conversation with people. She would sort of harrumph and look awkward and … It was pure agony for her to have to go out and socialize with people."

Elizabeth pauses slightly, and I see her brow working.

"And *all* … my … life," Elizabeth's voice clips out the words, emphasizing her disgust, "I remember hearing about her arthritis. Ever since I was very young. She went straight from childhood to having rheumatism and arthritis and sciatica and all those things."

No one, apparently, ever tried to pry Anthea from this hypochondriacal state of mind. She was always referred to as "poor, dear Anthea." My mother's tone of voice threatens to launch into a diatribe about my grandmother, so I steer her gently back to the manor.

"Do you remember any other servants? Did you have any favourites?"

"Oh, I remember lots of them," she chirrups. "I remember Richards, the butler. He was a great friend." She starts up again and I relax once more. "He took away my plate when I didn't want to eat the fat that was left over. I'd hide it under the knife and look at him and he'd hurriedly remove it."

I picture Richards with a kind, fatherly face, gentler than that of my grandmother and great-grandmother, and I am glad for this reprieve in Elizabeth's otherwise gaunt childhood. It feels less bleak to know there were some grown-ups who tried to make those early years easier for Elizabeth.

"How old was Richards?"

"Oh, he was probably about 40 or something. I don't know. He seemed to me sort of tall and thin and young with dark hair. And he used to go out shooting with Mother sometimes, which was kind of strange. She would get him to come along and then he could carry the various rabbits or pheasants, whatever."

I sit forward, wondering about the possibility of an affair between the dark, withdrawn Anthea and Richards. "Would they have been the same age, more or less?"

"Um, probably."

"And single?"

"No, no — there was a Mrs. She made me two dolls. Sammy and Susan. Sammy had a blue knitted suit and Susan had a pink knitted suit. And they had a double bed, which I thought was interesting …"

I pass over the telling comment about the double bed and return to Richards.

"So there were no kids for Richards and Mrs. Richards. You were sort of 'the' kid for them, I guess?"

"Yes. We didn't see Mrs. very much. She lived in a cottage up in the village, and he came down during the daytime. If there was ever a late evening of people staying, which was terribly rare, he had a little butler's room at the back of the house he could stay in, but otherwise …"

My attention slips as Elizabeth continues. The small possibility that my grandmother may have had an affair with Richards fades into a mere figment of my imagination.

"So," I ask again, "there was Richards and Frithy and … ?"

"Two parlour maids under Richards." She pauses again. "The head parlour maid stood at one end of the table behind Mother's chair while the butler stood behind Granny's chair all through the meal. So you could never really talk about all the gossip you wanted to talk about unless you spoke in French. Which is why a lot of people did in England."

I nod, remembering Molly, my eccentric great-aunt, and her sudden bursts of French during mealtime conversations.

"And there was a ferocious old cook who wouldn't let me eat between meals. She was a very good cook, but she was a miserable, grouchy old thing 'cause her feet hurt. She lived in felt bedroom slippers because, I think, she had bunions and corns and all sorts of dreadful things and she'd probably spent her whole life standing on a cold, stone kitchen floor all day. And there was a kitchen maid and a scullery maid."

"What's a scullery maid?"

"A scullery maid is an unfortunate human being who's probably about 13 years old, straight out of school, who spends her entire life scouring pots and peeling potatoes and vegetables and scrubbing kitchen floors and doing lousy things."

"What does a kitchen maid do, then?"

"The kitchen maid does slightly more elegant things. She's trusted to actually do some of the cooking and she tidies up after the cook, who *really* does the cooking."

"So does the cook order the groceries or did Granny May? Who did the menu planning?"

"Granny May interviewed the cook every morning after breakfast, about ten o'clock, nine-thirty maybe, with a slate. Sometimes the cook would come in to see her in the library, but usually Granny went into the kitchen. They would discuss the menu for the day, and possibly some of the things for the following day. And since nobody was entertained there very often by then, it wasn't a huge lot of decisions to make. So they discussed the soup and the meat and the pudding and the cheese and all these things."

"Would the cook be able to say, 'Now, Mrs. Firth, there's half a joint left over in the larder' or would she just say, 'Yes, Ma'am' to everything?"

"Being of Scottish descent she probably would have suggested the cold meat in the larder. But don't forget, we had all these servants to be fed in the hall, and they took about three times as much food as we did. Some cooks didn't feed the servants properly, then there'd be rebellions, you see, in those houses. So on Sunday, for instance, when we had the roast beef, it would be a huge sirloin with the tenderloin left underneath it. Mother would turn it over — she always did the carving after Grandpa died — and she would cut out the tenderloin and we'd just eat that and the rest of the roast beef would be whisked off to the kitchen as soon as possible, 'cause the servants were having their Sunday lunch too, you see."

"You *always* had a roast beef on Sundays? Always?" I am smirking as I ask this question, thinking of the hit-and-miss meals my mother served us most weekends, the way I cook now.

"Always!" she nods. "Then on top of the kitchen staff we had a Mrs. Hacking who came in from the village. She wore long skirts and boots and a big woolly hat on her head, and she was very fierce. Twice a week she scrubbed the whole of the back hall passage — oak floor, herringbone pattern — from the green baize door through to the front regions, all the way down to the back door."

"So who did the basic dusting and sweeping?" I ask, amazed.

"Well, that was the two upstairs maids." She says it almost disdainfully, as if surprised by my ignorance.

"Oh," I say, trying not to sound perturbed when I add, "You had upstairs *and* downstairs maids?"

"Two housemaids, yes." Elizabeth halts as if thinking about something. "And there was a vacuum cleaner in that house which was purchased when I was quite young, but I don't think it was ever used. Probably no one knew how."

Although this odd bit of information is interesting in some quirky way, I am suddenly overcome by an inexplicable feeling of guilt. I find myself sinking into the couch, once again appalled by the decadence of my ancestors' lifestyle. I know my mother wouldn't understand the shame I feel, or my disgust that so few people required so much domestic help.

"And there was a poor little housemaid," Elizabeth rambles on, "who used to get on her hands and knees with a dustpan and brush and sweep the upstairs carpet, which was a huge, wide hallway, all the way from the far regions, right round the corner to Mother's and my bedroom, every day."

I can hear my teenage daughter's righteous indignation to this piece of information — "Why didn't she tell them where to get off?" — and so I ask, "How many feet would that have been?" Trying, perhaps, to justify the job to myself as well as to my daughter's future criticism. But my head is full of the extravagance of hand-sweeping such a long hallway, and I cringe at the image of the unfortunate teenager, younger than my own child, born to such a ridiculous responsibility.

"Oh, about the size of this whole house," Elizabeth's hand sweeps through the air to indicate the good-sized rancher my parents inhabit, "or more. But I mean there was never a speck of dust or dirt there anyway! It was the sort of thing people did because they'd always done it, you know."

She sighs and shakes her head then, and I wonder if she isn't acknowledging some of what I'm recognizing, that huge waste of time and effort.

The thought makes me sit up and smile, a weight lifted off my back. I think again of the distance between my mother's upbringing and her present lifestyle and remember why she amazes me. I remember the two houses I grew up in, how they were full of mess and confusion, and there was rarely a fuss when something got spilled or broken.

Would I have coped with, even survived, the adaptations Elizabeth has had to make?

Family Secrets

At the opening of grouse season each August, Bernard and Mary Firth spent two weeks with the children at Moskar, their Derbyshire hunting lodge. On turning 13, each young Firth was taught shooting etiquette, instructed by the gameskeeper not to point a gun until taking aim and to "break" a gun not in use.

This was another rite of passage in the English upper classes and one in which Anthea showed keen interest. For the first time she enjoyed a shared social activity, that of scrambling over fences and running through rutted fields after prey with others. She must have hoped, when she came to marrying age, for a mate of similarly "outdoorsy" mind.

But Anthea's wedding at age 21 to Lancelot Hugo Humphrey Payne, a captain in the Royal Horse Artillery, was doomed from the start. Humphrey, who wasn't "in the picture even long enough to win a repeatable nickname" from the Firths, had been born in India in 1895 and sent to an English preparatory school in Bath. Humphrey rarely saw his real parents — "rather an unfortunate sort of way to grow up," Elizabeth says. Instead he was raised by Colonel and Mrs. Lea, his uncle and aunt, who lived near the Firths' home at Norton Hall in Sheffield. The Leas' only child had died in infancy and, according to Humphrey's son by a later marriage, Colonel and Mrs. Lea "lavished much on Father that he personally hankered after in later years, but never had the means for."

Humphrey was educated at Charterhouse and the Royal Military Academy in Woolwich. That and the fact that he was the son of a British army colonel destined him for a long and prestigious military career. "Being from the upper class," Elizabeth explains, "Humphrey was made a commissioned officer without having to work his way through the ranks."

Anthea met her future husband at a hospital in Dorset where he was recovering from the emotional devastation of his World War I experiences.

"He had been at Gallipoli and ghastly places where they were having bloodthirsty battles," Elizabeth tells me. I can tell by the rising tension in her voice that she is becoming sentimental about her estranged parent. When I remember my own father's war experiences, though, her overprotectiveness seems forgivable.

"He was only a very young man," Elizabeth shakes her head as she explains, "who'd grown up in a rather protected sort of world and was suddenly shot into an army and told to take charge of a battalion of men." I'm not sure by this comment whether to feel sorry for Humphrey or for the men who were slaughtered under his command.

Although Bernard and Mary didn't want "Baby" to marry Captain Payne, the explicit reasons why are now buried with them. "Perhaps they thought he was unstable, though socially the two of them were from the same class of people," Elizabeth says. Nonetheless, Anthea and Humphrey were married in Knightsbridge on November 5, 1921.

In one of only two remaining photos from their wedding, a London *Times* shot taken on the steps of St. Paul's in Knightsbridge, I recognize something about the groom. Though it's my first look at a grandfather I never knew, I've seen those ears before. A curious likeness of my brother looks back at me, as well as my mother's smile. In that first instant of recognition I wonder whose idea it was to destroy all the evidence of Anthea's wedding. Did they forget she would always have to face the living proof of her failed marriage in the eyes and smile of her daughter?

Below the photo is a list of wedding guests, names that sound like characters in a play. The Countess of Richester and Lady Mary

FoxStrangways, Viscount and Viscountess FitzAlan, the Hon. Magdalen FitzAlan-Howard and Captain the Hon. Henry FitzAlan-Howard, etc. The mouthfuls of titles continue for a full column of newsprint.

The professional portrait of the wedding party — the only other undestroyed photo of the event — is disappointing. Molly, usually the plainer of the two sisters, stands with beguiling serenity beside the bride. But Anthea sits as though weak of heart, with a strained look on her face. She seems stunned, distanced — shocked? — by the grin on the man beside her. The groom appears like a boy in men's clothing, and he and his best man stand stiffly, hands locked uncomfortably in front. The gargantuan sprays of flowers — the bride's bouquet of "palest shell pink roses and lilies of the valley" and the bridesmaids' "chrysanthemums shaded from yellows to autumn leaf tints" — tell me, more than the clothes, the jewellery and the numbers, that this is a family of means. The women wear veils, held in place by slender wreaths of flowers and leaves, looking like daughters of Christ.

When the Firths made it clear they "were not keen" for their daughter to go to India with Humphrey's army regiment, the young captain resigned his commission, a step his parents considered very foolish and one that immediately threatened his income. Consequently, the Firths set their new son-in-law up as director of the Leckhampton Quarries, another of Bernard's business interests.

But Humphrey was both inexperienced at business and completely lacking in financial acumen. Under his inept management, the profit-making quarry was eventually lost. This latter failure may have finally decided the Firths against Humphrey Payne.

And Anthea must have felt a great responsibility in the matter, as though the failure of both the marriage and the business were her fault. Not only had she been the cause of her father's loss of investment, but she was also the reason her young husband had given up his career. She was to carry the guilt of those burdens for the rest of her years.

Elizabeth was born in September, 1922, nearly 11 months after her parents' wedding. Her birth certificate names Yeovil, Somerset, the town nearest Clifton Maubank (where Bernard and Mary Firth moved after Norton Hall), as Elizabeth's birthplace. Humphrey is conspicuously absent in all of my mother's christening photos, taken when she looks to be no more than three months old. And Elizabeth is grim when she remarks, "I'm not too sure he was even around when I was born."

Over the years to come, what Elizabeth learned of her father from the close-lipped Firths were mere snippets of information.

She was told that Humphrey was known to have an explosive temper. Once, when Anthea had gone up to London, she met a brother officer of Humphrey's on the return train and travelled back in conversation with him. Humphrey reportedly flew into a rage over her behaviour, apparently assuming infidelity on the grounds of his own jealousy.

Perhaps Anthea had some starry-eyed ideas about marriage, my mother suggests, and felt unable to "put up with the sexual side of things." She also speculates that Humphrey may not have been a good lover. I am tempted to extrapolate from that comment but decide to accept its mention as merely a possible explanation for Anthea's failed marriage.

A trembling look on Elizabeth's face — a hesitancy lingering between tears and rage — pricks my attention. I hold my breath, recognizing in her expression that my mother still hasn't come to terms with Anthea's silence about the past.

"All I ever got," Elizabeth shakes her head bitterly, "when I asked about it was, 'Oh well, you know … it just didn't work out very well,' or something like that. Mother *never* told me. And nobody else would, not even my granny. She said the same sort of thing: 'It's difficult for you to understand, such a long time ago … ' Everybody sort of rambled off and this sentence just sort of faded away and one never quite got an answer to anything."

"Even Molly?" I ask. Surely my great-aunt, known for her forthright — even blunt — nature, had explained the problem of Anthea's marriage to Elizabeth.

"Well, I think when I was very young Molly probably didn't think it was *right* to tell me anything. Wasn't her place, or something. And when I was older she just said, 'Oh well, it was such a total disaster from the start and nobody really wanted her to marry him …'"

I am momentarily taken aback by a look of piercing intensity on Elizabeth's face. But the fierceness subsides as she resumes speaking.

"Maybe everybody but Mother could see that he was thoroughly unstable …" Her voice fades and she sighs.

Humphrey managed to get through a lot of Anthea's share of the Firth inheritance before they separated. "In those days," my mother reminds me, "you just handed it all over to your husband and he supposedly managed it. This is why Mother didn't have as much capital as Molly and the others."

Anthea and Humphrey's marriage officially existed for nearly three years, the divorce being finalized sometime between 1923 and 1924. But their time spent beneath a shared roof was less than one year.

Resting Places

When Anthea left Humphrey early in their marriage, she went home to her parents at Clifton Maubank in Dorset. And though Humphrey made attempts to re-establish their relationship, Anthea maintained her distance. A few years later, she and her daughter moved with Bernard and Mary Firth to Coates Manor in Gloucestershire.

When Elizabeth was four, Anthea and her daughter moved out of the manor into their own house in the tiny village of Coates. Barely a city block beyond the large iron gates of the manor, The Thatched House faced the south fields stretching away from Coates Manor.

"Perhaps Mother was tired of living with her parents or she wanted to have her own home, or maybe Granny couldn't stand having a small child around. Anyway, I remember walking up the road, pushing my doll's pram, the final piece of furniture to get moved from one house to the other. And we lived there for only about three years because in 1929, when I was seven, Grandpa died quite suddenly. He got pneumonia and died in about ten days, which people did in those times because there were no antibiotics for pneumonia.

"I can remember being at the manor and everything was rather hushed, and there was a nurse in a uniform rushing about, you know. And we were all very quiet and 'mustn't make a *sound*,' etcetera, which I understood. And then I remember a frightful row one day because Grandpa's nurse used to take her dinner and meals with us.

The maids refused to serve her at the dining room table because they said they weren't waiting on people of their own class. And Granny said, 'You WILL!' And they said they wouldn't, and she fired whoever it was, you know."

Moving back to Coates Manor after her father's death, Anthea became the epitome of the good Victorian daughter. According to Elizabeth, "Every time Mary wanted something done, 'Anthea'll do it,' she'd say, and Anthea did it."

Mary dressed herself in black for the requisite number of years after her husband's death and, even five years later, only ventured into purple, grey or mauve "in a very quiet way." Sometimes, Elizabeth remembers, her Granny May would wear black-and-white print dresses or dresses trimmed with small amounts of white. But she considered herself the "poor widow" and continued to use writing paper with a black border for many years. By this time in her life, Mary had done with socializing and was content never to entertain again. Anthea, who wasn't social at the best of times, was happy to live quietly with her mother and daughter, avoiding visitors of any kind.

This was the atmosphere in the huge Georgian manor house where Elizabeth was raised.

"The local morgue," she says, and grimaces.

After Bernard's death, Mary Firth tried to maintain her exorbitant lifestyle, staying on in the large manor house and keeping an enormous staff. During the Depression, though, her standard of living was cramped by shrinking dividends from the crashing stock market, and she found herself overextended. Mary's sons, concerned about the costs of running Coates Manor, asked their sister Anthea to pay room and board for Elizabeth and herself. "Anthea was already managing the entire household, ordering supplies and making most of the decisions about the things needing doing on an estate of some size," but she agreed to help with the cost of servants and her mother's lifestyle by contributing a monthly wage from her substantially drained marriage settlement.

By this time of her life, Mary, who had always been short, was quite fat, spending most of her day in an armchair and never taking any exercise. "It was always rather shrouded in mystery, but I think that after having five children everything internal had sort of dropped and she suffered, rather, from calamities of one kind or another."

So Elizabeth's Granny May sat for most of her later years, not complaining, but never moving very far away from her armchair. "She just tottered gently onto the patio for a few minutes — except you didn't call it a patio. That was considered a silly, modern word. The terrace — she went out onto the terrace — and had Mother do everything for her."

Looking at the last photos taken of Granny May, I can see how much Elizabeth resembles her grandmother, how little like her mother she is. Much rounder and softer than Anthea, she admits she has her Granny May's build, fat and fleshy. But she must have her father's eyes, because there is no trace of May's blankness or Anthea's sadness there.

She also has a very different temperament from Anthea's. Elizabeth wrinkles her nose and can look a bit cloudy when she dislikes something, probably a hangover from the days when she was to be seen and not heard, but Anthea's ire was something to hide from. If the gardener had done something other than what she'd requested or the washing-machine repairman hadn't come when he was supposed to, my sister and I knew better than to make our presence obvious. Granny Payne could easily reach a boiling point over something held inside too long and then we two girls would have to creep upstairs to wait it out, monitoring Granny's heavily lopsided gait as she paced in anguish across the flagstoned hallway. Peering through the banister railings, I'd see the smoke of a cigarette — like a cloud billowing from the top of a volcano — curling over the grey head of hair below.

But when inevitably the gardener had to be dealt with or the errant repairman arrived, Anthea avoided a verbal tirade. Instead, as befitted one properly brought up, she addressed them with such disdain and coldness it was impossible to misunderstand her meaning. Her displeasure at having to deal with anyone so impertinent and so common as lackadaisical workmen was evidenced by the insidious disgust with which she treated them.

Anger is one of the emotions that hovers around my family, especially the women, wreaking havoc with their faces and tracing lines of tension across their brows. It is unnerving to see in the mirror the heritage of those faces, the combined expressions of my parents and even some of my grandmother's. Their mirages look back at me with some — much — chagrin.

For some years now I have tried to concentrate on not frowning or sneering when I speak, on becoming sensitive to even slight twitches of facial muscles. Nonetheless, two permanent vertical creases in the area between my eyebrows — lines I never saw germinate but which have rooted nicely during the past quarter-century — tend to dominate my facial expressions. My father wears the identical two furrows on his brow — the Brown permafrown.

Perhaps it's the flawed genes that are dominant in families.

One Big Happy

*S*pread over my work area are the pictures, letters and diaries, even some favourite recipes of my dead English relatives. On the wall in front of me, the precise black lines of the English family tree run back through the centuries to Agnes de la Penne and Radolphus de Domer, 1166. My mother is the librarian of this family history, rattling off different stories whenever I ask about a certain name, storing records in her memory as her mother and grandmother did before her, records that will be lost with her death, like the identification of all those stern faces in the many photograph albums I have inherited. And I am overwhelmed by the size of my history, the magnitude of my family and my small place in it.

But all these ghosts I've exhumed with such fascination are only names now, their pasts constructed through mail and obituaries, the family annals. And Great-Grandmother Mary Lewton Firth and her daughters, lead players in the stories told during my childhood, have attached themselves to me like an inherited disease, part of some inescapable genetic program. In comparison, the history of the Browns seems unbalanced, effaced by the obvious lack of letters, photographs and heirlooms. The Browns are less substantial, less believable, almost as if their ghosts wanted no part of posterity.

Over the years, the two family backgrounds have remained unblended; a point has never been found where the attitudes and cultures can comfortably intermingle. Elizabeth's worldliness has always seemed diametrically opposed to Eric's hardness, their discordant union surviving only to counter each other in what has become a three-generation ritual. Sometimes my parents seem like a microcosm of contemporary Canadian politics, reluctantly accepting each other's differences only until the status quo is threatened.

One day Eric finds an old metal box, dented and with a lock that looks as though it has been crowbarred, and he opens it to show me its treasure: old photos, dance programs, newspaper clippings. Mementos from another era.

His fingers tremble slightly as he leafs through the contents then pauses to squint closely at something. He lifts a photo from the box, then shows it to me. "Here's Mother when she was very young. Isn't she beautiful!"

It is not a question, and I smile indulgently, expecting to see a photo of Elizabeth, but when I look at the face in the picture, I am confused. This man who has always referred to his wife as Mother — Mother of his children, Mother of our household, Mother of all time as though there were only one Mother in the world — shows me a black-and-white photo of someone else. A millisecond passes before I understand that the woman in the photo is *his* mother, the grandmother who died when I was 18 months old.

The photo of Eileen Sophie Weldon is an odd size, maybe two inches by four inches, and well-crumpled, perhaps from being kept in a shirt pocket or a wallet. A plain-looking woman in a large-checked dress, Eileen stands in an unkempt garden, scratching a cat behind the ear. The cat sits on a wooden frame where six good-sized fish hang in ascending size, but neither the cat nor the woman seem interested in the fish. I look at the woman and smile encouragingly at my father, wondering if it was his hands or his brothers' that made those loving creases in the picture. I open my mouth to agree with his praise but stop, seeing him lost in his thoughts, unconcerned by either my presence or my opinion.

He hands me the photo and continues rummaging through the box. Once again I inspect the face of the grandparent who died before I knew her, searching for evidence of the stories told by my mother and aunts.

"Old Eileen never cared much about the boys," they have often said, referring to my father and his two older brothers. "She lived mainly for her bridge parties and social functions. The boys pretty much brought themselves up."

It is a harsh judgment of the woman in my hands, someone who seems ordinary enough in celluloid. I look deeper, scanning for evidence of her criminal character, the cold mother who cared more for her own life than her children's well-being. The dark circles around her eyes and the large nose remind me of heartless Dickensian matrons, and I shiver, siding too quickly with Eileen's daughters-in-law.

I hand the photo back to my father as he finishes rifling through the contents and closes the box.

"You can take this home with you. Put it with the other stuff," he says. He is referring to the several files of papers he's already given me, a stack of unidentified photos, notes and letters about his foremothers and forefathers, pioneers of both the Maritimes and of Vancouver Island. He tells stories about them, stories whose impressive details change every year for more impressive ones, stories that make Eric sit a little prouder, a little taller, his chest just perceptibly swollen.

"My great-great-grandfather, Adam Horne, was the first white man to cross Vancouver Island," he beams at me. "There's a lake named after him somewhere over there." (Later, when I check the map, I find that there is indeed a Horne Lake just north of Qualicum Beach.)

"He married a full-blooded redskin, too."

"Oh really, Eric!" sneers Elizabeth. "She was only a half-breed, surely, and it's nothing to be proud of anyway."

He looks up at her then through thick lenses that magnify his hurt look. "Why not?" he wants to know.

I lower my eyes and concentrate on the pad of paper, the scribbled notes in my lap, struggling to find a question that will interrupt this potential argument.

"Well, it was just not *done*, was it?" my mother continues.

The competition for whose ancestors were better, more outrageous, is on. I hear my mother's disapproval and feel sorry for my father. My parents have very little in common these days.

One of the few things my parents have always shared is an interest in travel, and from my foggy cache of childhood memories is an impression that they frequently went on long, childless holidays, leaving their offspring in the care of a housekeeper-cum-babysitter. Elizabeth tells me now that my feelings of abandonment are only the paranoid imaginings of a child, but one year, I remember, they drove back east with the boys and left my sister and me to survive in the care of a stranger.

I might have been about five then, my sister just three or four. When I ask Elizabeth if she remembers where we — the two girls — were on that trip, she raises her eyebrows and shakes her head slightly, disclaiming any responsibility.

"Your father probably didn't want to drive such a long way with two wiggling children," is her explanation. It's a funny kind of hurt I feel in response to her remark. I understand, but still, I think to myself, still …

It was around the same time, I think, that Eric bought a brand-new Buick, fire-engine red with fins as sleek as a manta ray. In those days he'd bring home a new car every two years, surprising us during dinner while we poked and prodded at the vegetables on our plate. It was a welcome diversion when, in the middle of a meal, something dangerously shiny slid off the road and onto the driveway.

We'd stare at the unfamiliar car coming up the steep drive, squinting at the glint of sun on its cut-wax reflection oozing round the wide curve toward the kitchen windows. And when one of us recognized our father behind the wheel, we'd stand and shout, chairs teetering and forks scattering peas across the black-and-white linoleum.

When that flame-red Buick slipped beneath the carport roof, we leaped as one from the table, abandoning dinner in the race to be first to touch the car's obscene glare. We sat on the new-smelling vinyl, squabbling over whose turn it was to pretend-drive until dusk, when Elizabeth dragged us off to bed.

When I go to the library to find a picture of that Buick, I learn that the year was 1960. I am surprised by the crudeness of the car's lines, out of sync with the conservative hemlines and tight hairdos of those days, remembering, when I stare at the coloured plates in front of me, the hard attitudes of that era, the rough emotions, words and actions that even an eight-year-old girl could identify from the other side of the wide, deep windows of those Detroit wheels.

The summer of that new red car, my father rented a trailer for an extended driving trip. My mother referred to it, even after being corrected by us, as a "caravan," saying, "Annie, take this box out to the caravan for me, there's a good girl." And I'd go out to the trailer with pictures of camel trains in my head, climbing through the flimsy aluminum door into the compact space inside and pretending to be in a Bedouin tent, unpacking the sheets and towels into the little cupboard and organizing pots and pans for the long journey across the desert to the next oasis.

Maybe that was the summer they drove east with my brothers. On that road trip they saw Yellowstone Park, Mount Rushmore, Niagara Falls and New York City — the Empire State Building, the Statue of Liberty. I remember a long, tense week of preparations for the trip, and I wonder now if that was partly because my father likes to maintain control of everything, barking orders like a sergeant-major while my mother gets fussed by his continuous string of commands and takes her frustration out on whoever happens to be around — in the way — at the time.

By the time they were actually ready to leave, there was a sense of both relief and anticipation at their departure. Father pasted on his fake smile — the one that told me he was in a hurry to be on the road, heading out, but he knew he had to go through the niceties of goodbyes first — and Mother sat beside him, breathless (with exhaustion or excitement?) and smiling as the Buick pulled slowly away.

I remember my sister and I standing with our babysitter at the top of the driveway, wagging our hands after the car in case one parent or the other should turn and notice us. We watched as the Buick and its load crept slowly down the driveway to the road. Then the flaming-red car turned a curve in the tarmac and instantly the sound of crunching metal and breaking plastic rose above our loud goodbyes.

"Goddamn it!" my father's voice funnelled back up the driveway. We listened to the clunk of the car's gears being slammed into Park and we shivered in anticipation of what his anger meant, each of us glad it wasn't our fault.

My father's wiry frame emerged from the driver's door and he stumped to the rear of the car. The sharp point of the right fin had pierced the trailer's metal siding, simultaneously breaking the tail-light's plastic cover as the car turned. The Brown permafrown rippled across Eric's forehead as he limped back to the car and slammed the door, putting the car into Drive once again. But as the car disappeared, Elizabeth turned to wave at us gaily, somewhat incongruously, from the passenger window.

I've never been east of Idaho in the U.S.A., never been to New York City, and even now I wonder why I feel cheated by having missed out on that trip. It's not as if I'd remember any of it today, and I know how the road trip went: an early-morning start, a soggy, single-box serving of cereal to tide the boys over before a truck-stop brunch, the driving heat of the day leaning in one side of the car window, shoving elbows in the back seat and cross voices from the front, the bad moods that coloured some part of everyone's day. In reality I didn't miss too much.

And when they returned from that trip, there was a matched tear on the other side of the trailer, an identical wound on the left tail fin of the car.

Fraser Canyon Summers

My father's real legacy is the backwoods of British Columbia, the raw, uninvaded places where he took us on school vacations, filling us with the austerity and stillness of the country he loved. Those vacations always began with the endurance of the Fraser Canyon in July, the walls of rock sizzling on either side of the car as we snaked our way north through shimmering mirages on the melting tarmac.

We passed through the sizzle of canyon en route to the numb darkness of rain forest or the rolling dry of grasslands, all the different climates of British Columbia. Images tumble through my thoughts as I gather the memories, spilling and blurring into a vision of a rainbowed puddle at an out-of-the-way gas station where we stopped for fuel and Eric stood beside the pump, smiling and nodding as if he knew the overalled stranger there who pointed into the distance of those dusty roads. My mother would encourage us to get out and have a look around, but there was nothing out there beyond the endless roadside forest. For 13 summers I let this scene play out, and then I began to question the point of its routine.

Summer holidays, 1964. I am lying in a patch of sunlight in the over-cab trailer, rolling with each lurch of the truck on rough gravel. The movement tosses me like an absently rocked cradle, the warmth of the sun and the slow, uneven motion making me lazy. Bizzy is already asleep and I lay my head down beside hers, bumping above Eric and Elizabeth in the cab below us.

I wanted to stay home for this trip, at a friend's house, but Elizabeth said it was a family holiday and we were all going together. I sigh loudly, unhappy about this retreat to the middle of nowhere at a time in life when I should be going somewhere. The only girl in my grade-seven class who will spend the summer camping, I think about Mary Lu at her horse-riding camp and Kate at her family's seaside cottage. The continuation of disgruntled thoughts eventually puts me to sleep, and sometime later I wake with tousled hair and sleep-stuck mouth, hung-over eyes. When I look out the window, I see a familiar stretch of green. Again. It is the fourth night of our tour through northern B.C., and so far the small towns and empty countryside are not very impressive to my adolescent eyes.

The truck is stopped and I can hear my parents' voices outside. With a bizarre contortion of the neck I can see their shadows on the needle-carpeted ground, their folding chairs beside a fire ring. Through the trees is a stream, the branches of cedar lifting and dropping like the slow-motion arms of my city friends waving goodbye. The sun slants off the water and the reflection is harsh. Evening light. I must have slept.

The silence of the woods and the absence of distant traffic has wakened me every night of this trip. Scared of the dark out here in the wilderness, I call out for my parents though I am old enough to know my fears are childish. At night I stay close to my family, peeing where I can still see the circle of familiar faces reflected like so many moons in the lurid firelight. In the daytime I am aggravated and displeased by their company. My sister is stupid and babyish and my parents are embarrassing.

When we stop for lunch, I look around the restaurant, bored, as though I'm only with these people for the ride, a hitchhiker and not part of the family. Convinced that observers will intuit my outsider status by the obvious disparity between us, I reapply pale lipstick and run fingers through my long, straight hair to emphasize the point. At the cash register I stand away from Eric in his fishing hat and Elizabeth in her white shorts, the one sporting fishing lures and

European flags, souvenirs of other driving trips, and the other emphasizing blue squirms of cellulite and varicose veins. Gross.

Out here in the middle of non-stop wilderness, I realize I'm glad I wasn't allowed to bring a friend along. It's okay for me; I'm used to doing weird things like this with my family: cooking over a campfire, the pots and pans so charred that, if they rub against your jeans, the black stain they leave is permanent; washing dishes in streams lit by flashlight at night or hidden by mist in the early morning, the water too cold for soap to make suds and bits of food and fir tree needles sticking to the melamine plates and cups even after you've tried to dry them; strange meals of old cheese and salami from a cooler that smells so bad when you open it, you don't want to eat anything in there; lying in my sleeping bag and watching my father limp outside to pee. A friend would never understand.

It's Eric's withdrawn nature, his reclusiveness, that drives him out of the city from a life of law precedents and court trials to such a different existence. And I wonder about that oscillation between opposed ends on the continuum, about how he came to choose the tension of city life over the desolation of the backwoods, where he is transformed into another, gentler person. But I am too young to really want to understand the ways of adults and so I see only the enigma of this man, my father.

Eric's love of driving trips took us down narrow, dirt roads marked PRIVATE, looking for a clearing in which to have a picnic. One year on that drive up the canyon we stopped for lunch on a plateau just outside Lytton, following a steep, potholed track and coming out on an empty cattle pasture. The view of the Fraser's floor was spectacular, sickeningly dizzying. Instead of following my father and the dog to the edge of the cliff, I helped with setting out the picnic — sandwiches, fruit, beer for my parents, pop for us.

When the dog started barking hysterically, I looked up to see my father throwing rocks and backing away from something. The dog's tail wagged, but he was crouched in an attack position. Ruggles was always finding ground squirrels on these trips, bringing home bits of fur and mangled sinew. Sometimes his catch wasn't yet dead, and my father would have to finish it off, wringing its neck or bashing its skull with a stone.

"Mother, get the gun!" My father's voice, especially raised, is imperative and undeniable.

Elizabeth found and lifted the .22 and some shells from the car trunk, hurrying across the field toward my statuesque father in the distance. When she came within reach, he stretched his arm for the gun and motioned her away. Elizabeth stood, arms crossed, the wind whipping at her skirt and hair as he loaded and sighted the weapon at the ground in front of him.

I watched him raise the .22, slouching his left shoulder into the butt of the gun and pulling the trigger with a sudden yell of victory. The dirt splattered out in a small tornado as the shot hit the ground and something long and dark was carried through the air. I turned away with a shiver.

We sat at our picnic with the remains of a rattlesnake, my father grinning like a young boy with his first trophy. Elizabeth passed sandwiches with a kind of breathless excitement and the infectiousness of the moment blanketed me with a sense of surrealism. Now it is an engraved image of time, caught like a Kodak moment, hanging in my memory like one more photo in my mother's albums.

When I am older, Elizabeth, sister Bizzy and I will go on a girls-only holiday, turning our backs on these northern camping trips and flying south instead, staying in Hawaiian hotels with ocean views and room service. The three of us will spend whole days reading, swimming and dozing in the sun, eating nothing but tropical fruit and acting on whims. It is an easy, relaxed time that drastically alters the previous standard of family vacations. But when the plane door first opens in Honolulu, the rush of hot air that sweeps up the aisle brings a sudden attack of nostalgia and the heavy memory of all those oven-like days in the Fraser Canyon. Childhood summers flash before me in a slow-motion replay of long-distance vigils: thighs stuck to vinyl upholstery, damp hair on flushed faces, hot tempers and bodies crowded in that over-crowded car, stopping only for meals or for Bizzy's constant carsickness, otherwise going straight through, my father behind the steering wheel, driven. Even if we had to pee, we held it as long as we could in order not to annoy him, distract him from the goal of getting there. The feeling at the end of the day was another kind of exhaustion, of defeat perhaps, as if travelling was our duty.

I use those early road trips to map my youth. From a distant memory of a campsite near Blue River or a mid-afternoon swim in the Ashnola, I fill in the missing bones of my childhood, trying to make connections with some old black-and-white snapshots taken by Elizabeth during sporadic attempts to record more family history. Those photos, like the network of B.C. highways, red and blue lines criss-crossing a washed-green background of road map, are the ligaments of my beginnings.

A battalion of Douglas firs and western red cedars struggling up blank mountainsides, the alternately trickling or storming waters pelting over granite to Pacific shores, the marine smells of the wharves and beaches in small seaside towns — these are the spillways of the legacy left me by my father. And it is not until much later in life that I will understand how my memories of those Fraser Canyon summers bind me to my father's land.

Measures of Worth

*A*t what point do we turn away from our parents in utter revulsion at their weaknesses? And at what point do we return in recognition, perhaps acceptance, of our own human foibles?

When Elizabeth tells me about her youth, I am ashamed. So many times I've accused her of being an ineffectual adult without stopping to consider the lasting effects of her young years. Much of her childhood was spent wandering through solitude, companionless but for the estate farm animals and the occasional servant. She longed for other children to play with — friends — but because the social experiences of a small child weren't an important consideration at Coates Manor, she had infrequent opportunities to develop the social graces she needed. It was an exquisitely designed torture for a girl whose future was invested in society.

⁓

There were, in Elizabeth's early years at Coates, rare visits from her cousins, Mark's children, but after the two families' nannies disagreed, Mark's family stopped coming to the manor.

"There was a dreadful fight behind the green baize door, about when the pudding should come up from the kitchen or something." The green baize door, a thick slab of oak covered in dark, heavy silk, separated the back wing of the house from the front, the servants from the family.

Elizabeth's nanny was in charge of ordering meals for Coates' nursery, so when the visiting nanny overstepped her authority by speaking to the cook, harsh words and threats of leaving were flung about the kitchen. Mark and his family never came to stay — or were never invited to stay — at Coates again. Throughout such domestic crises, Elizabeth's predicament was never considered.

Left mainly to herself then, Elizabeth played imaginary games in the acres of fields or the large back rooms of the house. Her favourite haunt, especially on rainy days, was the large box room above the coal cellar, itself "the size of a triple garage in which an enormous truck dumped the coal twice a year." Both box room and coal cellar stood at the far end of the house, behind the servants' quarters.

The box room was a repository for suitcases, bunches of dried flowers that hung from the ceiling — mostly lavender, but sometimes roses, chrysanthemums or hydrangeas — and a full regalia of different-sized boxes. Round hat boxes, large, flat dress boxes, long, thin cigarette boxes and every other conceivable size of container were stored on the ceiling-high shelves of the room where Elizabeth was allowed to play as long as she didn't make a mess. She shrinks down, shrugging her neck into her shoulders, and tells me sheepishly, "I sometimes did, you know ..."

But I have deserted her, left her alone with this moment as memory carries me back to Coates Manor, wandering its long-desolate hallways in search of the rooms my mother so intimately remembers here today. And I am aware, once again, of the sharp emptiness I felt inside the old house, seeing the desecration of the nursery, the linen room, the box room. The way ornate ceiling mouldings loomed from the austere heights of rooms that felt as big as Kitsilano bungalows. It's hard, now, not to imagine the solitude of a small child playing in all that blank space, alone.

In the fields next to the manor was a herd of Jersey cows, "more sociable than most; they'll stop and talk whereas the other kinds run away." The image I have of the young Elizabeth hanging from a fence, chin resting on top of the stone walls, dark bobbed hair with its trademark bow — "I *always* had a bow pinned on the side" — is forlorn. I see the oversized brown eyes and wet, dribbly noses of those Jersey cows and wonder how responsive they were to the young girl.

The estate had many places for a child to indulge her imagination or hide from the adults. The old coach house, an empty building used to store apples all winter, was a favourite because of "its lovely smell." And the summer house, a miniature Grecian temple in the shady corner of the garden, was a perfect respite in the spring and fall when it was too cold for the adults to take their tea outside. There was also Beech Cottage, a two-room playhouse built to replicate the one Anthea and Molly had as children and placed at the far end of the manor's gardens for Elizabeth, "so the noise wouldn't disturb my granny." But Elizabeth's only regular playmate was Bobby, the Highland terrier whose life is commemorated by a watercolour painting variously hung in the homes of my mother, my sister or myself because no one has the heart to throw out the woodworm-eaten bequest. And Bobby, though a steady companion, was more interested in rats and voles than in Elizabeth's childhood games or later true confessions.

Over the high stone wall between the manor house and its farm was a 15-box stable. Riding, an inherent part of country life, was encouraged from a very early age, and at three, Elizabeth was put on a pony and led about the paddocks.

Elizabeth's Uncle Phil was the local Master of the Hounds, and so she learned to ride in anticipation of that controversial ritual, the fox hunt. It was an expected rite of passage, and in their youth both Anthea and Molly had ridden to the hounds, sitting sidesaddle ("it wasn't *ladylike* to ride astride") on big bay hunters, long skirts over their britches, veils over their top hats, protection from splattering mud.

At Elizabeth's first fox hunt she was given the brush (the fox's tail) and bloodied (marked with fox blood) to initiate her into the exclusive club. She didn't worry about the apparent cruelty of setting so many hounds against a single prey, never felt sorry for the fox. "The hounds demolish the fox in a matter of *seconds*," she emphasizes, "'cause they're all so starving hungry. They're not fed that morning, you see, before we go out."

I smile at the way she speaks in the present tense, pleased that the memory is so alive for her today.

"I mean, these people feel so sorry for the fox, but the fox, once he's caught, he's gone — phht! — just like that." Her thumb and forefinger pinched together, she raises her hand like the wisp of smoke from an extinguished candle.

"How many hounds?"

"Oh, a couple of dozen."

"How do they share one measly little fox between them?"

"Don't know! Not too many people are right there when it happens, you know …"

Amazing, to me, that this lover of animals could be so unfeeling about a fox. Her horse was another matter.

Though Anthea and her siblings traditionally had their own horses — a gift from parents or, as in Phil's case, a passionate hobby that consumed money — none of the horses in the manor stables belonged to Elizabeth. Instead, Anthea rented a pony for her daughter to ride during school holidays.

Snowy, a fat, placid animal leased from Elizabeth's boarding school, would arrive by train at the Coates siding, a stop that "existed mainly for strange bits of freight: horses or sacks of coal, the odd piece of machinery."

On the tracks in the middle of the silent Gloucestershire countryside, the source of the famous Thames bubbling out of a deep welt in the ground below, Elizabeth would wait impatiently, jumping on and off the rusting rails, throwing stones down the bank, listening for hints of the approaching train. Holding her arms out for balance, stepping gingerly along the steel-rail tightrope, she passed the time pretending to be a circus star, filling more of her empty day, waiting. And when the chuffing engine slid into view, drawing up beside her and halting with an impatient snort of steam into the noncommittal blue sky, Elizabeth took Snowy by the halter and led him from the freight car, neck balking and whiskered lips muttering at the indignity of his passage. The two old friends stood by the siding and shared a moment of greeting, nuzzling and stroking before Elizabeth rode Snowy the few miles back to the manor.

Anthea rode regularly with Elizabeth in those early years, but a later hunting accident forced my grandmother to stop riding altogether. Afterwards Elizabeth rode with Mustoe, the groom, but "he was too old for a vigorous gallop across the fields; a bit boring."

During the winter months at Coates, Elizabeth would be invited to children's fancy-dress parties, and she would go as a "Red Indian" or a Dutch maid or as Granny May's hero, Lord Nelson. One year she was a fairy, "with frilly skirts of bronze and gold that stuck out and a wand with a star on the top." No homemade efforts these, Elizabeth's costumes were either rented or purchased from a London specialty shop — "horribly expensive."

The guests, children of the local gentry, were escorted to the parties by their nannies, who sat in a row around the edge of the room while the children were entertained. "They were supposed to watch to make sure we didn't slop ice cream or kick somebody else in the ankles or forget to say 'Thank you very much for the nice time,' but they probably had a glorious gossip!"

Elizabeth was chauffeured to these events in Granny May's Daimler. She sat in the back of the huge car with a fur rug over her knees and a foot warmer beneath her shoes, a glass partition between the driver and herself.

"I felt like royalty arriving at a party, and I'd be rather embarrassed 'cause not many other children were sent in anything quite so grand."

Jackson, the chauffeur, was another of Granny May's throwbacks to better times.

"He was much fancier than anybody else's chauffeur," Elizabeth says. "Everybody had a chauffeur in those days, but they usually wore just a dark blue uniform with a dark blue peaked cap." Jackson, though, wore a cream-coloured uniform with maroon trim, the jacket's silver buttons impressed with the Firth lion-rampant crest. My mother shakes her head. "I think Granny May just hadn't moved on since the time of Edwardian coachmen."

But Jackson was also a friend to Elizabeth, despite the class separation between them. Because parties were a frightening experience for the young girl, unaccustomed as she was to so many companions and so much activity, Jackson would help out if she wanted to leave a party early. When she was too old to be any longer accompanied by a nanny, Elizabeth would tell Jackson, "Please don't be too late coming back," and he'd be there waiting when she made her escape. "It was the panic of being there and wanting to come back, you know." She looks at me doubtfully, as if I couldn't possibly understand.

When she was eight, Elizabeth was sent to a small boarding school in a neighbouring town. Connie Harrison ran Mathon Court House for "about six little girls besides her own two daughters, and we all stayed in their red brick Georgian house" near Malvern. Mrs. Harrison was the wife of the man who ran Bernard Firth's estate whenever he was away on business, and as Anthea was friends with Connie, it seemed natural to send Elizabeth to Mathon Court.

"We went riding and we went out painting pictures with our sketchbooks in the pony cart. We studied art and we learned quite a little bit about music. And we marched about with bean bags and wooden bowls on our heads to keep us upright."

"Deportment," I interject.

"Yes, precisely." Elizabeth nods. "And we had wonderful French lessons from a funny old lady who came once a week, walked all the way down the hill from Malvern, and she brought lovely picture postcards with Margaret Tarrant's pictures of fairies and elves and goblins and animals and flowers, which I've always loved, and we would discuss these pictures in French, and if we did well enough, we got to keep the postcards."

Elizabeth tilts her head, looking into the distance of her memory. "And we walked up into the woods and picked wildflowers." She hesitates briefly, frowning at something, before resuming jerkily. "But Aunt Connie sort of … She had a dislike for me and everything that went wrong seemed to get blamed on me. Finally my friend Johanna told her mother that Aunt Connie wasn't very nice to me, and I guess her mother told mine because next thing I knew Mother came over in a rage and took me away and that was the end of that."

When I ask her what kinds of things were blamed on her, Elizabeth can't remember more than an incident when something got dirtied and Connie yelled at her. She was ten and a half when she left Mathon Court.

"And then what?"

"Then I went to a real school — Sentryfields — in Swanage. That was a proper boarding school: uniforms and all that. They were dark brown, and I've never worn brown since."

At Sentryfields there were six different forms, with six to eight girls in each, and they slept four to a dormitory. The seven other girls with whom Elizabeth "went all the way up" are still good friends.

She lists the subjects studied at Sentryfields. "Music, Art, Dancing, English — literature and writing essays — History, Maths — of a sort, which I hated and couldn't understand — French. And then after a while, because I hated History — it was terribly boring — we were studying the Industrial Revolution and the Franco-Prussian War and I just couldn't have cared less — I liked the German teacher so I managed to wiggle out of History and do German, to my mother's horror. I loved it." She grins at me. "Oh, and Latin," she suddenly adds.

And at Sentryfields Elizabeth learned more about real life. In the dorms after lights out, the girls tried flashing mirrors to signal the boys' school across the road. They sneaked food in and shared it with each other during whispered gatherings in the dark. They waited 'til they thought the teachers were asleep and had pillow fights. And to get even with the teachers they hated, they'd creep into the faculty bedrooms and put effervescent salts in the chamber pots or lean out the window at night and dribble water on teachers' heads as they passed beneath. "And someone — can't remember if it was Doreenie or Maureen — taught me this." Elizabeth swallows a gulp of air, then opens her mouth to produce a loud belch.

I stare at my mother in shock before noticing the gleam in her eyes. Then we both laugh at her uncharacteristic behaviour.

The girls rose early at Sentryfields, sharing a jug of water between two washbasins. If their parents had paid an extra fee for music lessons, as Anthea had, the girls practised piano at 7:00 AM in the unheated, stone-floored practice rooms for the half-hour before roll call and breakfast, which was "mostly just cereal and bread and butter and marmalade. *Sundays* we had grapefruit, big hot fresh rolls and marmalade. But on Saturday night the food was awful because the teachers weren't there, so they gave us whatever slop they had in the kitchen. Big jugs of yellow stuff — we called it Tom Cat's piss. Supposed to be lemonade."

The school grounds were surprisingly barren. "There was a *tiny* garden; you couldn't go and sit outside or lounge around. We spent our entire life either in the classroom or walking up and down to the playing fields which were a mile away."

Introduced to new sports at school, Elizabeth excelled as an athlete. She was captain of the school lacrosse and netball teams as well as a key player for the school's tennis team. "Which wasn't hard considering there were maybe six tennis players in the entire school!" But the weekend tournaments against other schools provided the drama of the week, and Elizabeth and her friends looked forward to the matches played throughout the school year. Other than that, the only activity they had was an enforced daily swim from May to July. "They marched us down to the beach and we changed in tents on the shore, and they made us go into the water for a good 20 minutes or more. It was always freezing, but it was considered good for us."

During school holidays, it was to Anthea's sole friend in Coates, a widow with a daughter the same age, that Elizabeth turned for relief of boredom. "Dorothea always had room for just one more and we'd go out on little picnics and things like that. And we did things like making toffee at her house which I couldn't do at home because the cook was an old grump. I wasn't allowed in the kitchen."

"Which was more boring, then, being at school or being at home?" Elizabeth doesn't hesitate when she answers. "At home."

~~~

Elizabeth had dreams of one day riding in a point-to-point steeplechase. By the time she was 15, the age when she could have entered the sport as an amateur, Anthea had stopped renting Snowy in order to save costs.

It was a crushing time. "I minded very much," Elizabeth says, and her head sags with the weight of the memory so that I can see the child's downcast face, the slow rolling tear on a smooth cheek. But then her neck jerks and her head is tossed back quickly as the words become adult again. "Perhaps the Depression was affecting the family more than I realized. I mean, people never talked about money, and certainly not in front of children. Anyway — just the way it went." Elizabeth turns away from me, and I can no longer read her eyes, supplement her words with something nonverbal.

In her own reserved way, Anthea tried to expand her daughter's life. She took Elizabeth on vacations: to Cornwall after a bout of chicken pox; on a camping trip with Uncle Phil, towing a caravan through small seaside towns; to Switzerland with Molly. In Switzerland the three of them rode a cable car to the top of the ski hill, sat in the sun and drank apelsaft, then "piddled around among the trees 'til we got down again." But Anthea only skied once or twice, and the rest of the time Elizabeth and Molly kept each other company, skiing, skating or going for sleigh rides.

It wasn't that Anthea didn't enjoy being a mother, but more that mothers of her ilk and era didn't normally bring up their own children.

"You just had them, probably." Elizabeth shrugs as if to remove any blame, but her facial expression is one of guarded doubt.

Motherland

We look at the albums of carefully preserved turn-of-the century photographs: childhood portraits of Molly and Anthea in frilly bonnets and pinafores, long skirts and lacy blouses, enormous hats and parasols.

I turn the pages and watch my English grandmother and great-aunt growing old before my eyes. The last photos of the two sisters together on the front lawn at The Thatched House make me ask, "Why did they both wear their hair in such harsh, tight curls?"

Elizabeth sighs again, shakes her head. "They didn't have any imagination about hairstyles or fashions at all, I don't think."

When did they trade the kid-leather pumps for oxfords, the silk dresses for tweed suits? How did they escape that predestined prescription for ladyhood?

"I used to be so embarrassed," Elizabeth sighs. "Mother always wore tweed skirts and those huge, flat sort of men's walking shoes." Now her voice drops to a whisper and her head shakes disparagingly. "I used to just about die …"

I shrink into the sofa, remembering when I too felt embarrassed by my mother. As a schoolgirl, I was mortified when Elizabeth spoke in front of my classmates. Their eyes would widen at her funny language and they'd tease me later, or tell someone else how she said *biscuit* for cookie, *woke* for walk and — the all-time gut-buster — *yaws* for years.

For years (*yaws*) I was so over-sensitive about the difference between other, normal mothers and my own that I purposely avoided telling Elizabeth about the closing ceremonies for various courses. I didn't want her to be there, to congratulate me within earshot of anyone who didn't already know I had such a strange background. These days we can joke about my youthful reactions, but I still regret that early treatment of my mother.

A hard edge creeps into Elizabeth's voice. "And then some of mother's friends dressed the same, had this masculine ..." Elizabeth hesitates, looking for the right word. "... *outlook* on things. It was almost as if Mother had a tendency to dress this way so as not to look feminine and *silly*, so as to look like her big brother Phil and all things masculine." Her voice underlines certain words with a tone of deprecation, pure disgust, and once again I wince at the harsh judgments of a mother by her daughter.

"Why weren't you embarrassed by Molly, then? Didn't she dress the same way?"

"She didn't somehow look quite so *man*nish. I couldn't explain it to you. I didn't even know there were such things as lesbians then, but I wonder if Mother was gradually developing towards that?" Elizabeth looks at me with a kind of despair, a certain helplessness that wants me to ridicule her suspicions.

Ignoring her plea, I ask, "Or was it Molly's extroverted personality that made you more able to accept her as she was?"

"Oh, yes. Yes." A leap at an opening.

The Vancouver rain drizzles down the glass of the living-room window, obscuring the dense green of cedars and golf course, the temperate northwest climate outside. It reminds me of so many rainy days at Coates, of Anthea at her bay window overlooking the vast spread of fields disappearing into distant valleys, and now I wonder when her zeal for life was crushed.

As she aged, Anthea began to face life with the glum conviction of a prisoner, her sad eyes like those of someone condemned. Was it because she had expected a husband would take care of her? Didn't she believe it possible to do for herself?

After her divorce, Anthea initially tried to maintain the privileged lifestyle she'd always known. But when she found herself with a substantially reduced income, no husband to produce a larger one and no home to call her own, she was forced to change her expectations. She began to see herself as the victim of some inescapable martyrdom and withdrew even further from all social situations. Especially next to the ebullient Molly, Anthea began to appear moody, resentful maybe. Those moods were something Elizabeth had to live with.

But Elizabeth, determined not to be restricted by the depressing world at Coates Manor, made concerted efforts to expand her social experience. "I don't know if I was very good at it at first. I remember being awfully awkward, going to dances and having to talk to people beyond the half a dozen or so that I knew well. I felt like an ape, hands hung all the way down to my ankles on each side. I didn't feel very gracious at all."

In her late teens, Elizabeth reacted to the fact that Anthea never returned party invitations. Though her mother excused herself by saying that "Granny May was not keen on parties," Elizabeth dug her heels in and insisted on throwing a bash for her young friends. After a closed-door conference in the drawing room, Anthea agreed that Elizabeth could hold a dance at Coates Manor.

"I wore this much-too-grand dress that mother's friend had given me, which she'd worn at court or something. It was a pink — almost salmony pink — net with a skirt that went out from about here downwards," Elizabeth holds her hand sideways at her thighs, "and it was all very modern."

They held the dance in the main reception hall, a 70- by 25-foot room with four arched alcoves of ornately carved plaster and ceiling frieze, a large marble fireplace at one end and a carved mahogany staircase at the other. An extension of the entrance hall, the reception hall was probably never meant for a dance, but in preparation for the party the carpets were rolled up and the furniture packed away. "We danced there because the floor in the drawing room, which is where we should have been, I guess, was considered to be unsafe. It was over the cellar, and we 'might have all fallen through,' which I thought was absolute rubbish! They probably didn't want us using the furniture or something. But it was a lovely house, and you could have had marvellous parties and dances there, really."

My mother's face is wistful as she talks. She sweeps her arm, fingers arched like a ballerina as she describes the enormous entrance hall that flowed into the party room with its large fireplace. She danced all night, the slim brunette in a salmon-coloured dress, whirling across and around the black-and-white marble floor to the unusual strains of a band in Coates Manor. And because she was the hostess, Elizabeth danced with each of the young men at the party.

Her eyes shine as she relates this last piece of information to me. It is, perhaps, Elizabeth's only fond memory of that time of life. When her peers were presented at court, Elizabeth, despite being landed gentry, was excluded from the great whirlwind of social events. As a divorced woman, Anthea was not allowed to present her daughter.

"It was a funny rule left over from the Victorian era. Queen Mary was a pretty sticklish old lady to whom divorce just wasn't an accepted status for women. Things like that wouldn't have been allowed in her time."

Queen Mary's rules only corroborated Anthea's self-doubt. In her own eyes, my grandmother felt that divorce had made her into some kind of social oddity, that her failure at marriage somehow proved she was not quite acceptable in "real" society.

Missing the presentation at court was a huge disappointment for Elizabeth. It was a rite of passage that all young women of her social level looked forward to and from which she felt cheated. She shows me the photo of Anthea taken for her presentation in June 1920. The young girl holds a large ostrich-feather fan in front of her dress, creamy beaded satin with an above-the-ankle hemline, white silk stockings and satin pumps, a Grecian hairstyle and a corsage at her waist. On the back, Mary Lewton's handwriting reads "*Anthea, before Buckingham Palace presentation to King George V and Queen Mary. Dress by Reville, court dressmaker, London, W.*" The most eye-catching feature is my grandmother's youth.

"What was so special about curtsying to the King and Queen?" I want to know.

"It meant you went through a marvellous month of parties here, there and everywhere all over the county. You got asked to a dozen or so dances in this short space of time; you were invited to other people's country places for a weekend or a week or a day or whatever. You were sort of *launched* into society in general."

I tell her that it sounds like a very competitive thing, the kind of situation where girls often try to outdo each other by being the belle of the ball. Elizabeth laughs.

"It's different there, not like it would be here. Here everything seems to depend so much more on money and what you can prove you are. There it would be lots of debutantes turning up in weird dresses made by the local dressmaker because the mother, the Duchess of Somewhere, really couldn't care less. She's quite likely very much more interested in going hunting!" Elizabeth shrugs and cocks her head, amused at the truth of the situation.

Though she wanted to escape the morgue-like atmosphere of her family home, Elizabeth's presentation at court would have assured that she continued in the circles of her grandmother's society, a society of long-nosed judges.

"It was terrible, really, when you think of it now. If you looked at the sort of shoes people wore, you'd know if they were a lady or not."

"What? Not really!"

She nods quickly. "Or the kind of gloves they wore. People did *not* wear cotton gloves. You wore *good* kid gloves or nothing."

"So, if you wore cotton, what did that mean?"

"Common, cheap. If you were *really* a lady, you had good shoes and a good handbag. It wouldn't matter if they matched, necessarily, but those things were important. And there was something about a voice. I mean, I couldn't tell you now anymore, for I've been away so long, but I would know *exactly,* when I was young, by somebody's voice, whether they were really out of the top drawer or not."

I wonder, as my mother speaks, how much of what she says is left over from her grandmother's influence. Elizabeth has repeatedly described the character of Granny May as a strong Victorian woman in front of whom "I didn't dare say the wrong thing or speak out of turn."

Neither did May have a reputation as a warm employer: "She was either very intolerant or she didn't pay the maids well enough," Elizabeth says, "because none of them stayed very long." Perhaps they reacted badly to Mrs. Firth's dictatorial manner, but whatever the reason, most of the girls moved on after a fairly short time or they were fired because they were "no damned good."

It is interesting, considering those comments about the dark side of Mary Lewton, that Elizabeth's best childhood memories are of times spent one-on-one with her grandmother, learning how to sew and play cards. Elizabeth remembers Mary's favourite game, Bézique, as being played with two decks from which cards below seven are removed. And though she's never heard of it since, she insists the game was "all the rage" in the '30s. Today the double leather card box with BEZIQUE embossed in gold on the top is still in my family, all set up for the game that none of us know how to play.

But for my mother's memories, that leather box would be just another souvenir from a forgotten past. There are so many of Elizabeth's stories that astonish me, make me question more and more of my heritage, especially the one she now relates about millinery rules.

"My dear," Granny May once insisted, "whatever you do, *never* buy a pink hat." Elizabeth smiles before continuing in her grandmother's voice. "Doesn't matter who you are, it looks common."

"What's a suitable colour of hat, then?" I ask, mystified about these never-learned women's secrets.

"Oh, anything else, I think, but pink," Elizabeth assures. Then she stops briefly, considering something, and adds, "Cream's good."

"What about yellow? Or green?"

"Navy, blue, brown," Elizabeth continues before hearing me. "Yellow *might* pass. Green, I don't know … Mmm, at Ascot, perhaps, but *not* anywhere else."

This is what my mother brought with her to Canada.

Apples and Oranges

*R*eplaying the interview tapes, listening to questions and answers about my English relatives, I have intermittent jolts of recognition: even after four generations there are undeniable similarities in family personalities and characters.

I think of my sister, how both our daughters bear an uncanny resemblance to the English side of the family. My own daughter looks remarkably like the young Molly, while Bizzy's daughter is a replica of the earlier Anthea. And my sister's approach to life is much more like that of our easygoing great-aunt Molly, while I am like our grandmother, a woman less able to embrace and relax into the world, always trying to orchestrate some order, design a manifesto for life.

Just so were Anthea and Molly quite different. Though Anthea was frequently embarrassed by Molly's loud or overly blunt comments, it was my great-aunt's forthright nature that rescued Elizabeth from an otherwise bleak life. The one source of light in an invariably cold family, Molly's smile still brightens the dark pages of the Firth photo albums. And it was Molly's zest for life that enabled Elizabeth to find an alternative to the dull existence at Coates Manor.

Molly must have recognized, in a sisterly way, the potential damage to a child by a mother who saw herself as a failure. Very early on, Molly assumed the role of Elizabeth's second mother, having her niece to visit on holidays. Then, when Elizabeth went to boarding school, Molly came for her "most religiously" on the two weekends per term her niece was allowed off school grounds. It was Molly who taught Elizabeth how to socialize.

After completing her regular schooling, Elizabeth had a year at a domestic science school in Lyme Regis, spending her weekends with Molly. "She was always having people in for drinks. She'd get me to come and help her put out the sherry and the nuts and the potato chips and the olives and I thought this was great fun. I'd never done anything like this in my life because we'd never had parties at home, you know. And Molly was so relaxed about it; there was no fuss about preparations or anything, but it was exciting for me. I used to love going there."

When she pauses, I know Elizabeth is remembering, trying to access something for me to understand.

"See, at home I'd always had this feeling I did everything wrong," she begins, and then stops again. "My poor mother," she sighs. "I guess it was her air of authority that I could never quite duck."

But in Molly's company Elizabeth could be herself without fear of making a mistake. And Molly, who'd married a man with an already-grown family and had no children of her own, cherished Elizabeth's company in equal measure.

"Why didn't she have kids?" I wonder aloud.

"She just decided she never wanted any," Elizabeth says.

I am skeptical of her pat answer, asking instead, "Did they use birth control then?"

Elizabeth nods. "Oh, yes."

"Diaphragms?"

"I think so. Don't know, but they had something. Yes, definitely."

"But wouldn't that generation of women have been uncomfortable — uneducated — about such things?"

"Not Molly! She wasn't shy about *anything*!"

I have my doubts about the reliability of the birth control available to women in the 1920s, but ask instead about Molly's stepdaughters, wonder if they were resentful of their father's young wife, only slightly older than they were.

"Didn't the children worry about further siblings with whom they might have to share an inheritance?"

"According to Molly they were all good friends." Elizabeth smiles in fond reminiscence. "I don't think Molly ever had any enemies, really. She was more just the eccentric kind of person that everybody thought, 'Oh, poor old Molly — she's a bit mad, you know!' But his kids were quite fond of her, I think."

Molly married first in her late 20s. Being "an older bride" gave her the time to have "a wonderful life, tearing around with young people and other friends." But Molly was unlike most other women of her time: an extrovert with a quick sense of humour, she was not what most young men of her social class wanted in a wife.

She met Martin Hughes, husband number one, in 1925 when "young women were flipping out doing their own thing, rather like the 1970s here." Elizabeth raises her eyebrows at me reminiscently.

"Would that have been a rebellious stage?" I ask, ignoring the eyebrows. "Molly going wild, striking loose from the family ties?"

"Perhaps. And I think they had a slight fit when she said she was going to marry this old geezer, you know."

"How much older was he?"

"Older than her father."

In 1925, Molly had decided she wanted to see the world, and she bought a ticket on a cruise ship, sailing gaily away, single and unchaperoned despite her parents' strong disapproval.

In Vancouver, where Molly decided not to disembark — the small town "didn't look very interesting. Nothing but a few wooden houses and trees" — she sent a wire home to England to say she was getting married. A second wire, sent a week later from the Panama, refuted the first, but when the ship arrived back in Southampton, the wedding announcement was published in the society pages of *The Times*. Molly's fiancé, one Martin Hughes, was not only older than her father, but not in the best of health.

"So she married this old guy in her late 20s and he was what … 50?" I ask Elizabeth.

"Oh, he must've been 50 or *more*, yes. He already had two grown-up daughters who were older than Molly. One was Deidre, who married a Baring of Baring's Bank, and the other was Lorna, who married one of the Kepples. You know — King Edward VII's lady friend?"

The name-dropping makes me smile; my mother loves to slip back to the society she left behind.

Molly had a "proper" wedding with all the appropriate trappings for a bride of her status. They married at St. George's in Hanover Square, London, where all society weddings were held "because you invited all your grand friends and they all had somebody they could stay with in London."

This information fascinates me, and I reminisce about my own weddings, the traditions so closely followed on such a minor scale. In retrospect, I realize both ceremonies were modelled on correct English protocol. Brushes with the past.

I make some snide remark about marrying at St. George's in Hanover Square in order to attract the richest and best of English society (along with their generous gifts) and am confused by Elizabeth's genuine surprise.

"I don't think the gifts or the being seen mattered so much. It was the fact of convenience for your friends from all over the country. It's easier to go to London than to expect them all to come down to the country. You'd have to find them all somewhere to stay."

Then she turns to me with a sudden question: "You remember Dorothea?" My grandmother's friend in Coates. "Dorothea was a nice person, sweet and kind, and she'd have everybody to lunch. She hadn't got a farthing, but she was accepted everywhere and her children were invited to everything because they belonged to that sort of crowd and they were likeable people. Nobody cared whether they were rich or not or whether they returned the hospitality. You knew they were somebody's poor relation so you were just nice to them. And really, they were much more blue-blooded than we ever were. She has all sorts of relations who are lords and dukes and earls and this and that, but you'd never know it."

"But they don't … didn't have any money," I frown at her.

"No, they didn't have any money, but her father was an army officer and her mother was the daughter of the previous Sir Somebody-or-other Brumhead, and Lord Birdwood was her uncle. He was the Viceroy of India, for heaven's sake." Elizabeth sits back in her armchair as if this explanation ends the matter.

"What happened to the money?" I want to know. Impossible for a person of knighthood or title to be poor. "Did it get gambled? Did it get spent?"

"I guess so. Just disappeared anyway, for one reason or another."

"But they were invited to all the social things, the gala affairs in the area?"

"Oh yes, absolutely. She's some relation of the Somersets who go back in history to Plantagenet times. You know, the Duke of Beaufort and all that crowd. They're all related. And Lord Raglan and Lord … um, Diddly or Something-or-other, in Scotland. I can't remember. But she never talks about it."

"Is that a rule of thumb then? If you are somebody, you don't talk about it?"

"Quite, yes."

"But there must be people who talk about it." I'm thinking of some wealthy Canadians, the ones who drive flashy cars and spend their days entertaining or going to spas, who never contribute to society except when it's to their benefit.

"But they're what I call … who's that ghastly woman that writes novels?" Elizabeth's face crumples into a frown of concentration as she digs in her memory. "Princess Diana's step-grandmother. You know — Barbara Cartland. Those sort of people talk about it."

"I don't know her," I admit.

"Oh she's a frightful old woman with false eyelashes like Mae West and pink hats and a painted face and she writes dreadful sort of romantic novels."

"Well, is she someone or isn't she, according to the rules?"

"No, she's *not* anybody."

"But she thinks she is?"

"She's just a ghastly Johnny-come-lately."

"Meaning nouveau riche?"

"Yes, of the worst possible type."

"What's the worst possible type?"

"Well, the ones that are so blatant like that. I mean, you could be nouveau riche and get away with it ..."

"And still be accepted in society?"

"Yes."

"In *upper* society?"

"*Just.*" She pauses, but only for a millisecond. "'Specially if you give nice dinner parties and have a yacht, you know. It all helps." She laughs and I'm back where I started, confused about the importance of money.

She tries again, taking me back to medieval England when the knights and their squires, the sons of local noblemen, had property with big homes surrounded by farms and/or villages which housed the lesser people who worked for them. "To preserve these bigger homes, the daughters were married off to somebody who had property and money, and in that way family incomes were kept intact and the control was maintained by the upper classes."

When people like Uncle Mark gambled away money and became penniless — compared to their former financial state — they could still retain their social status because of a certain quality or educational background. "They were brought up to *know* the proper rules of society," Elizabeth assures me, "and were therefore acceptable in certain circles, not just speechwise, but their whole way of life."

We're back to that unfathomable dictum: the innate, not-completely-teachable (therefore ultimately inaccessible to foreigners) rules of English society. It's like the game of cricket, I realize: a complete understanding of strategy and regulations is only possible when one is born and raised with the game. The rest of us are destined to stand on the sidelines in wonderment and disbelief.

"So how did someone come to be introduced to that society if she wasn't from it?" I ask.

"It was always possible to *do*. All through history people managed to gain favours either at court or in local social groups and gradually infiltrate. And I can think of people who were just not ... quite, quite, quite ..." Elizabeth stops and I raise my eyebrows at her in incredulity. She shrugs and continues.

"But they tried very hard and more or less made the grade to be invited to those functions and parties of a group that they didn't *really* quite belong to."

"Was it a matter of time, then? Did you have to prove yourself over so many months, years, parties, whatever?"

"I think you could do it by being very charming, and you could entertain people who were just a tiny bit more important than yourself."

"But would they deign to come?"

"Oh yes, I think so, if you were a nice person and interesting and invited other interesting people to your soirées or your lunch parties or your tea parties."

"But you had to have the initial connections to meet them first. You couldn't just send out the invitation not knowing them?"

"No, but I think even today there are people who ... hostesses, say, in London or here and there who are clever enough to invite an interesting group together. Not just intellectuals, but a cross-section of people, and they manipulate the conversation in such a way that everybody finds something interesting in another person. They work at these things, *make* people move around and meet everyone by excusing themselves and deliberately steering guests about. It's part of the art of being a good hostess."

I picture my mother in her younger years, hostess at one of the many parties she and my father held, wonder if she enforced this kind of mingling; wonder if, as a guest, being steered toward someone I "should" meet would make me balk, or if a society with such convoluted rules would ever admit me.

I think of Aunt Molly, honest and straightforward, and wonder if she recognized the farce of her society. The way she was dollied up for all those early photos, dressed in a bonnet smothered in bows, a very plain girl trying to look pretty, beside her delicate little sister who looks lovely, though somewhat lost, in lace and frills.

And it's the eyes, something about the eyes, that tell me how different the two of them always were. In all her photos Molly looks ready to run hurdles, her dark eyes impish and determined, Anthea's timid and forlorn. My daughter's eyes, my niece's eyes.

Perpetuated Lies

*A*t the death of her first husband, Hughes, Molly's easygoing nature was sorely tested.

"Hughes went mad suddenly in the middle of the night and attacked her. Clubbed her over the head or something. She had to call an ambulance, and they carted him off to hospital and he died. He had a brain tumour or an aneurism or something. They were always perfectly good friends — he just suddenly went bonkers."

Four or five years later, Molly married again. Guy Knight, her second husband, had been a friend of Hughes, all three of them members of the Broadway, Worcestershire, hunting crowd and society. Knight was another widower, also with two grown children. When he and Molly married, they sold their homes and bought The House on the Green, an old home in Broadway where my sister and I, when we were perhaps ten and twelve years old, were taken for lunch one day. And because we were Elizabeth's children, Molly made a great fuss of us.

She told us, as she heaped slices of cold jellied tongue on our plates, that the salad and the boiled new potatoes came from her own garden. But my sister and I, products of the post-war baby boom, were connoisseurs of the new North American processed foods, and Bizzy, a picky eater at the best of times, turned pale at the notion of eating anything quite so intimate as a tongue, let alone fresh vegetables. It was the kind of gastronomic offering over which she could only gag, and I saw her look helplessly to my mother. When I too barely nibbled at my food, Molly said nothing, only whisked the plates away in time for dessert.

I remind my mother of this luncheon, remembering aloud how at ease Molly was in her kitchen compared to Anthea.

"My dear, Molly couldn't boil an egg," my mother corrects me, frowning at my fallible memory. In the seconds of shock that follow, I recheck my memory, following images of my owl-faced great-aunt around her kitchen. I look again at my mother, see a hint of disgust on her face and wonder if Elizabeth is wanting me to acknowledge something: the adaptations she's had to face, the distance she's come from that same background. The changes she made to ensure her own survival.

The image of Molly as Donna Reed — chopping, stirring and mixing by the light of the garden window — fades into a blur. I am momentarily dumbed by the inaccuracy of my memory.

"I think Mrs. Somebody-or-Other would've put all the food out," Elizabeth announces in the middle of my hesitation. "Molly probably just had to bring it in from the kitchen. No," my mother reiterates, hammering at the flaw in my memory, "she wouldn't have known how to prepare a meal."

"So," I falter, "*neither* of them knew what to do in a kitchen?" My voice has a touch of awe in it, disbelief.

Elizabeth's head tips back and she laughs. "No!" And a second time, sadder, quieter, "No."

"But," I screw up my forehead, "how did Anthea learn?" And a split second after, "How did *Molly* learn?"

"Molly never did!"

"Molly never did?"

"No, I don't think she ever made a meal."

My head swims. Granny Payne in her kitchen in the early mornings, pouring corn flakes from a box, taking a fresh pint of milk from the little door in the wall where the milkman left two each day, thick layers of cream on top. "What did she do in the mornings, then? Just have cereal and milk?"

"Mmm ... she *might* have made a piece of toast ..."

"Was this a standing joke, then, that Molly couldn't take care of herself in the kitchen?"

"No. Nobody did from that generation."

And now I remember something else. Granny bending in front of her "cooker," peering worriedly at the bacon under the broiling flame. Her pleased relief whenever I came for the weekend, took over the kitchen duties, cooking and washing up.

"But Granny learned," I insist.

"Only she learned latterly in The Thatched House those last ten years. She boiled an egg. Then she fried sausages, I think. Bits of bacon sometimes. And then she used to take old chicken legs from a leftover roast; she'd roll them in mustard and put them under a grill. And then I think she learned to fry kippers, grilled kippers. Then maybe lamb chops. That's all she ever did, about five things like that. She wouldn't know how to roast something. And she wouldn't ever have peeled a potato — *ever!*"

A sudden sympathy for those two incapable sisters overtakes me. All the fun we made of their pompous British mannerisms seems cruel now, and I hesitate over the niggling guilt and shame of not having been more understanding. The memory of Molly, especially, standing on our front stoop so many years ago, intense brown eyes and embarrassing eccentricities, makes me wistful.

"So Granny ..." I hesitate, still lost in the confusion of shame. "In terms of taking care of herself, was Granny more advanced than Molly?"

Elizabeth's nose wrinkles while she judges the truth of that statement. "Slightly," she begrudges. "Yes, I suppose."

"Was this a great crisis, then, to have to learn to take care of herself?"

"Absolute agony. She loathed every moment of it. It was beneath her to have to go into a kitchen and do things." I avoid hearing the whisper of disgust in Elizabeth's voice, understand that it is a natural phenomenon, this mother-daughter rivalry.

Gently, gently, I pry at the feelings.

"This is what I'm trying to get at," I explain slowly. "Was it beneath her in terms of class or was it because it was scary? Did she see herself as being incompetent on *all* levels because she didn't have any of the necessary skills to be independent?"

The shoulders shift and the neck twitches. "I suppose you could, to be kind, call it 50-50, yes."

"Because the winter I spent over there, I remember Granny being quite ..." I search for the softest way to describe the memory of my grandmother's gathering distress, cords of tension rising on her neck whenever the bank statement arrived in the morning mail. And when I find a word, I breathe it out, only slightly relieved. "She was traumatized by the banking and household accounts ..." I let my voice trail off again, let my mother remember her own mother in those last years.

And when she speaks next, it is quietly, with an almost-sadness for the woman toward whom she still carries some anger. "She thought she hadn't any money ..."

"Yeah." I shake my head in sympathy.

And Elizabeth nods. "I know ..."

I am just beginning to realize how overwhelming it must have been for someone like Anthea to put up with us while we were young. It must have been a terrible dilemma when Elizabeth called to say she was coming for a visit: desperately wanting to see her daughter again but dreading the onslaught of those noisy, disruptive Canadian children who perennially accompanied Elizabeth.

Our sticky fingers at meals and our noisy demands at bedtime must have been particularly unsettling for someone from the old school of childrearing. When tantrums arose, Anthea would make herself scarce, walk to the bottom of the garden or somewhere she could better avoid the situation, dampen the volume.

"She wouldn't have known how to deal with it," Elizabeth says.

Most of my memories of Anthea are in sharp contrast to those of Elizabeth. I remember my grandmother as being interested in, although sometimes impatient with, the four of us. Perhaps our mother's slap-happy manner of raising a brood fascinated as much as appalled her, because Anthea was quite fanatical about the way certain things were to be done. Elizabeth, for instance, had been made to sit on the "throne" after breakfast until she *did* something. "Because if you didn't go, something awful would happen to you. You'd get stopped up for life or something!"

She and her mother couldn't have been more different.

"You mean you don't know whether they've *been* or not?" Anthea once asked her daughter.

Elizabeth shrugged. "No. Haven't got the slightest idea. I never ask them."

To her credit, Anthea tried not to interfere. Instead she kept her amazement to herself, only commenting, after Elizabeth's shocking revelation, "Oh, well. I suppose if it works for you …"

And Elizabeth, still full of rebellion, couldn't resist pointing out, "Well, it seems to. They're all still alive."

London 1940

While my mother and I remember Molly, we step to and fro, dancing with history and comparing different memories of the same incident. What we find is both nostalgia and fiction.

Elizabeth has saved Molly's collection of scrapbooks, full of picture postcards, programs for special events and other souvenirs from her life. On one page I find newspaper clippings: *Mrs. Guy Knight wins second prize at the Tewksbury Flower Show* and *Local resident wins at Broadway Flower Show.*

"Molly loved growing things," my mother says, noticing what I'm reading. "It was a great pride of hers."

I'm remembering Molly's prize narcissi, the quilt-like squares of chocolate soil and full yellow blooms laid out behind The House on the Green.

"Anthea was very scornful about Molly's daffodil prizes." My mother's voice interrupts my thoughts. "She used to say, 'Molly goes out and buys the very latest creation of some new variety, so of course she can win a prize. Other people can't afford to do that.'" Elizabeth thinks Anthea's attitude was sour grapes.

I scrutinize the face full of derision and think about how different her two mother figures were. How hard it must have been always playing her aunt against her mother.

Elizabeth's year at domestic science school in Dorset was an immersion in studies meant to prepare girls whose expected futures included a "good" marriage and the management of a large household.

"It was a sort of stopgap for people who had finished regular school rather early. You weren't old enough to do a lot of exciting things, but you might as well be doing something, so they taught us how to run a very elegant household."

"Very useful," I mock, but Elizabeth doesn't notice. She's gone, back into her albums of memory.

"We cooked *marvellous* things! We had turkey stuffed with pheasant or quail with pâté inside and truffles and glazed things over the surface and the whole thing had to be boned. It was the sort of thing you'd feed a banquet for a visiting president or something. A very good training. And then we had to do laundry. We put tablecloths and the local church linen and all the linen from the house into big boilers, as they called them, and just cooked the stuff. Poked it around with a big stick and hauled it all out and stuck it on a line to dry. And then we had little pot-bellied stoves with sort of rails around them and you put flat irons on to heat?" She looks at me quizzically to make sure I understand, am listening at the very least.

"And if you weren't careful you burned huge holes in things, which wasn't very popular. And everything was starched to the hilt!"

I am puzzled. "It doesn't seem appropriate for young women of the upper class if they were supposedly going into a home with lots of servants."

"Well, the idea was if you couldn't do these things yourself, you wouldn't know how to train the help."

"Wouldn't they come to you already trained?"

"No, lots of the village girls came straight from school, anywhere from age 14 or 15, and most of them were utterly clueless."

"Your mother did this too?"

"Well, no, but my granny did. And the real joke was, when I did start housekeeping for myself in Oxford, living in digs, we were under wartime rations. All we had to eat was dehydrated scrambled eggs from the U.S.A. — they came in a package and tasted like sawdust — two lamb chops once a week, two ounces of butter, two ounces of sugar, half a pound of tea and hardly ever any milk. It wasn't really in keeping with this *cordon bleu* stuff we'd been taught, you know."

"How were they able to teach you to cook with rationing in effect?" She looks at me as if I'm quite incapable.

"That was just *before* the war. We had lots of everything then. And it was all very basic. They brought in enormous, horrible-looking fish from the harbour with heads and tails and eyes and everything — guts — in them, and we had to clean these monstrous beasts in the kitchen sink and it was just disgusting. And they made me clean a chicken. I stood there with tears streaming down my face, pulling out unspeakable things from its innards."

"Could you do it again now?"

"I think if I were on a desert island I ... No, I don't know if I could do it even then."

"And so you've had this wonderful education — fit for the wife of a head of government — and you've never used any of it?"

When she shakes her head, opens her eyes wide and bites her lower lip as if slightly ashamed, I can see the young Englishwoman in that black-and-white engagement picture again, full of surface spunk, no guts to speak of. Those came later.

But Elizabeth has other memories to report, and she hurries me away from my thoughts.

"After domestic science school — that was in the winter of 1940 — I was still six months too young for war service, so I took a secretarial crash course."

The course was held at Stanway House near Broadway, the Worcestershire town where Aunt Molly lived. Elizabeth shows me a photo of the Inigo Jones gate house at Stanway, the arched stonework leaping over the main drive to the house, and she points out the window where her room was in that house, tells me how the water froze in the glass beside her bed at night.

"And I used to cycle over to Aunt Molly's to get a free meal every now and again."

"Wouldn't they feed you at the school?"

"Yes, but it was rationing and wartime." She pauses, and something in her expression tells me to wait quietly for her. Elizabeth's grey eyes fog over with memory, and after a moment of silence she speaks again. Softly. "I was there when all the men came back from Dunkirk, when they retreated from France. And they filled the whole parkland around the house there …" Her finger traces through the long acres of grass surrounding the old house in the photo. "Army tents everywhere and these men in rags, exhausted and really demoralized and …" She stops, bites her lip, and her eyes sink, the smile lines fading into sorrow. "It was a terribly sad time. We realized England was in very bad danger at that point."

Her voice drops as she speaks, lands on a hushed tone, and I tense, trying to hear every nuance of the feelings she is reliving. Nineteen thirty-nine and 1940, the beginning of the Second World War, the war most people thought would be the last great war but wasn't. Only a precursor to the explosion of Korea, Vietnam, the Persian Gulf and now Afghanistan.

World War II, the war that is too long ago for most of today's boomers to remember, but which lives on in my mind as some kind of romantic era. And while contemporary filmmakers are busy enshrining the period of my youth — the '60s and '70s — it is 1939-1945 that has become the time in history I would most liked to have lived.

~~~

I lean forward, a small child again, following my mother into the past as she brings the war alive, alarming but exciting.

"When Britain declared war against Germany," she says, "I was 17 and a half, six months shy of enlistment age." The next half-year was filled with the secretarial course, nine months condensed into six, and then, when some of her friends from Stanway went for jobs with the War and Foreign offices, Elizabeth applied to both. The first interview — with the War Office — ended in a job offer for MI5, Intelligence, based at London's Wormwood Scrubs Prison. She went straight to Coates to pack her things.

"I was just so thrilled to get the hell out of there." She shakes her head as she remembers. "I went up to London to a boarding house at Gloucester Terrace and that was that. I never looked back, only went home occasionally for a weekend when I'd got nothing better to do."

She tells me about the bombing of London, makes it sound like a pyjama party. Every night Elizabeth and her roommates gathered books, American chocolate bars and their mattresses and went down to the basement of the boarding house.

My eyebrows rise inquiringly at this piece of information. "Not a bomb shelter? Just the basement?"

"Just a basement. Some people went and sat in tube stations, but they all smelled of pee and were full of crummy, lousy people and shrieking babies. You wouldn't want to go down there, really."

I don't even hear her callousness. All those war movies, I am thinking. All those worried faces huddled underground. All that propaganda.

"I thought *most* people went down there. They didn't then?"

"No."

"Just a few people then?"

"Mm-hmm. And if you were out in the street and there was an air raid, the policeman would try and make you move along. He didn't like you just standing around on the sidewalk. I remember sitting down on the curb in the West End, eating an apple or something, and the policeman said, 'You can't sit here and do that.' And I said, 'Well, I've nowhere else to go. Can't go back in the shop' — they closed all the shops, you see — 'and I don't want to go home again. The raid will probably be over in a few minutes.' 'Well, you can't sit here!' he said. I had to walk away and go somewhere else."

All those terrified faces sardined in the stairwells of the Underground, shoving their way through the blackness, and my mother is sitting here telling me they weren't real. She films a different movie of unabashed youth eating red apples on brown London curbs while sirens wail and grey buildings crumble around her, sparing both apple and apple-eater.

It can't have been that easy, I think. "You mean you actually stayed on the street during air raids?" I ask, probing for holes in her story.

"Yes."

"But I thought everybody made this mass exodus to the Underground … ?"

"Well, you did and you didn't. I mean, half the time, by the time the sirens were shrieking, the planes had already been and gone. You never quite knew, really."

And because she seems so blasé about it, I can't resist a bad pun. "Sounds awfully hit-and-miss to me!"

But Elizabeth doesn't hear me. She's back in that movie as it flickers toward the climax. "And then sometimes in the mornings they'd start raids just as people were all going off to work, just to upset everything. We'd have to change the tube at Shepherd's Bush to get to East Acton, and the sirens were going so we'd have to go all the way home again!"

She looks incensed at this bit of inconvenience, and I laugh at her assumption that someone on one side of the Channel or the other deliberately scheduled air raids to upset the commuters en route to or from work. Elizabeth's notion that wars should be fought according to some universally accepted code of ethics seems naïve. I recall her ferocious indignation when telling me how her father, captured at Dunkirk, was "*walked* all the way to the nearest prisoner of war camp, which the Germans were *not* supposed to do with the officers." The pathetic fallacy of her belief in wartime etiquette simultaneously touches and saddens me.

She begins to move quickly through her bank of memories now. "And one day my friend Philippa went home and found the house had been sliced in half and her landlady was *dead* in the bathtub. That wasn't very nice, at her age."

I ignore the obscure comment about age and focus instead on how the landlady died. "Dead from shrapnel?"

"Well, a bomb took half the bathtub and killed her."

I am dumbfounded for a minute, trying to compose the picture of half a body, half a bathtub, half a building. One side of each item solid and intact, the other side blasted out of existence. Gone. Destroyed.

But Elizabeth sails on once again and I have to hurry to catch up. "And one night there was a particularly loud explosion between us and … where your car is." She points out the living-room window at my car, parked some 20 feet in front of the house. After I look and nod, I lift my eyes to the green of the golf course and the tree boughs across the road, noticing the way the wind waves through them while hearing her voice and feeling how it pulls me back to London, 1940. "There was a great explosion in the middle of a geranium bed outside the house. That shook us quite a bit. And that same night was the one when the shrapnel came down through the ceiling into the top bedroom on the third floor, second floor, whatever it was. My bedroom was only on the first floor. But if this girl had been in her bed, she'd have been killed 'cause there was this great, jagged piece of steel sticking right in the middle of her mattress when we went up after the air raid. And all the windows blew out, so it was a bit drafty." She pauses and then adds as an afterthought, "A bit scary."

Something happens to me then, and I begin to feel as though I am watching my mother from a great distance, her hands moving as she describes something far away from the close air of this living room in Vancouver, 1999. The war — any war — is so distant. Her mouth opens and shuts quickly, forehead wrinkling and smoothing as she shows me her movie.

Now I remember crying in the darkness of a theatre while watching *Forrest Gump,* sliding down in my seat to escape the terrifying blasts of napalm and the whump of helicopter blades in Dolby Surround. The sheer horror of mud-splattered and tear-stained faces on young men afraid of dying.

It makes me want to ask Elizabeth, *How can you sit there and talk about the shards of steel, the half-bodies and the screaming sirens, without sobbing and collapsing in a mass of jelly on the floor?* And though I say nothing, she seems to intuit what I'm thinking.

"You didn't think about your mortality a lot. These air raids were happening; there wasn't a damn thing you could do about it so you just *sat* there until it was over." She stops, looks at me from the other end of the couch and says, "How about some tea?"

This is what I missed out on while growing up in the 1960s and 1970s: the ability to be practical, stoic — British — about my emotions.

Living in the Doldrums

The original Coates Manor is registered in the Domesday Book, but the present house is actually an amalgamation of two different buildings. Hams Hall, dismantled in Warwickshire and transported brick by brick to Gloucestershire, was re-assembled at Coates to incorporate the original, much smaller manor house in its design. The manor is typical of Georgian architecture, a flat grey construction unadorned except for the columned Palladian entrance and two stone lions lying with latent ferocity beside the east wing's large bay windows. Beyond the landscaped gardens are unspoiled views of timbered parkland and open fields, and outside the long north wing of servants' quarters is a traditional stone fence that prevented the jersey cows from putting their noses to the kitchen windows.

One Sunday late in 1940, after a lunch made from the weekly meat rations, the kitchen was full of the clank and bustle of cleaning up when the explosion of loud fireworks overrode the clamour. Craning her neck to see out the window, the cook noticed some small puffs of black smoke in the sky somewhere between Coates and the town of Cirencester a few miles away. When nothing more appeared, she sent the maids back to work, told them to get on with clearing the dining room.

Outside the main entrance of the manor, Elizabeth, home from Oxford for the weekend, watched with Anthea and Granny May as two planes flew antics overhead. The RAF Kemble station across the south fields regularly held training sessions, and so after a few minutes, presuming that's what they were watching, the three went back inside. As soon as May had retired for her nap, a tremendous *whumpf!* pierced the quiet countryside. Almost instantly, loud voices and confusion filled the house. Across the fields, farmers with pitchforks ran toward the manor while Richards, the butler, shouted into the telephone.

"A fighter's been shot down at Coates Manor. We need the AFS, quickly!"

Behind the doors to the servants' wing, bedlam broke out. Shards of glass, blown out of all the north wing windows, littered the kitchen and the storage room. The food in the larder lay beneath a sparkle of broken windows and voices outside the house rose in a panic as flames from the burning fuselage shot up the walls toward the roof.

Elizabeth, delegated to rouse Granny May from her bedroom, raced up the wide flight of stairs.

"I'm not coming downstairs for Hitler or any other damned German!" the dowager snapped at her granddaughter.

"Yes, Granny, you *are*. This is the one time in your whole life that you have to do what I say," Elizabeth insisted, delighted with her power. "Come downstairs right now."

With great reluctance and much muttering, May came down to the library on Elizabeth's arm and Anthea poured a glass of brandy to calm her mother.

"She was so irate," Elizabeth giggles. "She kept saying, 'Why did it have to land in *our* house with all the damned fields around here!'"

A line of neighbours and staff worked together, passing buckets of sand and water while waiting for the arrival of the Auxiliary Fire Service. By the time the AFS arrived half an hour later, it couldn't get through the blocked driveway. The local Home Guard — "all the men who were too old for the army got issued Boer War rifles with which they were supposed to look after Britain if we ever got invaded, but which they couldn't shoot anyway" — had arrived ready to defend their country against the Germans and then stood around, disappointed, when there weren't any left to kill.

"The four Germans in the aircraft were blown to little pieces all over the place." Bobby, the terrier, brought in a boot with part of a foot inside it; a hand was found in the chicken run — "It was not very nice, way out where the chickens and turkeys were" — and, during the clean-up from the fire, "bits of people were found on the roof. It was all rather grizzly and disgusting …" Elizabeth screws up her nose at the distaste and inconvenience of it all. The Germans, or what was left of them, were buried in the village churchyard and left there until the 1970s, when their remains were exhumed and taken back to Germany.

Elizabeth or Anthea saved the magazine pages of the *Cheltenham Chronicle and Gloucestershire Graphic* from Saturday, November 30, 1940. The photos show the remains of a Junkers 88, a small German plane with incendiary bombs, shot down over Coates by a young RAF pilot-in-training. The wreckage of the airplane was so complete that it's hard to recognize anything in the tangled mess below the blown-out windows and charred walls.

At the end of the day, when all the neighbours, AFS and RAF officials had left, and Granny May was back at rest, Anthea went with the cook to assess the state of the kitchen and the possibilities for dinner. In the middle of the room, on the large wooden work table, sat a huge bowl of eggs, completely intact. Nearby, the only other untouched item was the enormous cast-iron stove.

"But then it would have done for a battleship," says Elizabeth.

For several days after the accident an RAF sentry patrolled the area of scattered debris outside the manor kitchen, standing at attention with his rifle on his shoulder, guarding the site against would-be looters. The manor, meanwhile, was given special compensation by the War Ministry for all the food lost. "A great celebration," Elizabeth smiles. "Double rations for the week!"

Little Ironies

*W*hile the excitement of the burning Nazi fighter occupied the population of Coates in the fall of 1940, a listless boredom simmered in the mind of a young man on the other side of the world. With no clarity about what he wanted to study, my father had enrolled in the Faculty of Arts at the new University of British Columbia, struggling through his first-year courses with a painful lack of enthusiasm. By the fall of 1941 and the beginning of his second year, however, the war was heating up in Europe: the Battle of Britain had been underway for a good part of the year, and the German Luftwaffe had spent the spring in a concentrated air attack (the "Blitz") on London. So when his buddies told him they were going to enlist, Eric went along with them, aborting his second year of studies.

I sit down with a huge file of his military records. Eric doesn't like to talk about the war, doesn't like to remember the uglier details of that part of his past, so, rather than discuss it, he gives me this dog-eared file folder. It's as close as I'll be able to get to the details of those early years, and even then I have to overlay the black-and-white facts from the yellowed sheets of paper with interpretations of stories told by others. My limited understanding of the man for whom these military records were kept is a source of great regret for me.

He joined the RCAF because his older brother was already a regular officer in the air force and because, like so many of the young recruits, he had a dream of rising to the top, becoming a pilot. They sent him to Regina, where after his medical the interviewer noted, "The candidate has red hair and probably the characteristics that go with it." Later, in the same report, the medical officer wrote: "Mentality [sic] alert — education good first class at UBC. Temperament determined — thinks clearly, plenty of guts, responsible. Motivation good. Physical very good. Leg length suff. for Pilot."

I stare at that last line a long time, trying to read around it, unable to make any sense out of it. In light of what happened to him, the fact that the length of Eric's legs was noteworthy seems strangely prophetic. Later I am told that recruits with long legs were not considered for pilot training because of the limited space in a cockpit. Those with short legs were also overlooked because of the difficulty of reaching the controls.

Eric came sixth in his class at Initial Training School, and even though his commanding officer reported that "he is a trifle erratic and argumentative and inclined to shirk discipline," he was sent to Virden, Manitoba, for Elementary Training. There he "gave excellent promise in class" and was pronounced "smooth on controls and ... manoeuvres" and was moved to Dauphin for Service Flying Training. On the final report, Eric's chief supervisory officer commended him: "Distinctly above average. Young, keen and conscientious. Reliable and dependable at all times." The squadron leader, perhaps a father himself, added: "Enthusiastic and willing ... inclined to be high spirited and irresponsible but will improve with age and experience."

I try to imagine being 18 again, young and naïve about my mortality, and wonder if pilot-training school enabled Eric to make some sense of his life. As if being good at something could make him feel accomplished, worthwhile.

He trained on single-engine Tiger Moths and Cessna Cranes, practising dives and spins over the wide-open prairies, feeling the aircraft's response to his touch on the controls, his sufficiently long legs pressed against the body of the plane. Maybe he looked into the clouds of the blue prairie skies and thought about flying through the heavens, trying not to think about what it would be like over foreign lands in the dark, searching for a target. Maybe he and his buddies hoped it would never come to that, but they talked about getting "over there" and setting Jerry right. Even when, in the rear cockpit of a Tiger Moth practising spins at 3,000 feet, he saw the ground "right in front of me" before the plane crashed, severely injuring the pilot and knocking him unconscious, even then Eric didn't consider getting out, going AWOL to escape his inevitable future. I try to remember: he was 18; he couldn't have known better.

The Final Report on Pupil Pilot Eric Brown, AC2, ranked him above average at landing, instrument flying and formation flying. Bomber-pilot skills. He graduated, a year after enlisting, in the top ten percent of the class. On March 19, 1943, Eric received his pilot's wings.

He arrived in England on April 16 that same year to begin a series of training courses with the RAF. For the next six months he flew Ansons, Oxfords and Whitleys, the giant aircraft of the British military, on ground reconnaissance, advanced, operational and coastal patrol missions. Then early in 1944, Allied Command initiated a plan of all-out air attack on Hitler's main control points. Because bomber-crew casualties were high, new recruits were needed for the bomber-training course. Eric was recommended and sent to Skipton in Yorkshire with the 424th Squadron, where he was reported to be "An ex-AFU [Advanced Flying Unit] pilot of above average ability who experienced no difficulty converting to type (Halifax). A very keen captain with more than average control of his crew." At the bottom of the report, beside the last line which asks "whether candidate is recommended for four-engine bombers," Wing Commander Gunn has written a definitive "yes," adding, "Has volunteered and is recommended for employment in Pathfinders," the advance planes that marked bombing targets with flares.

In the RCAF mug shots of my father, his identification number held just below the gold braid wings on the chest of his uniform, I recognize the heavy brow of my sister's son, the shadowed eyes. Eric wears his peaked cap at a jaunty angle — trying to look rakish? — but it only succeeds in making him look thin, haunted. I picture him in his Halifax bomber, the cockpit a wall of glass open to the skies and German artillery, and I shudder. Even the ugly yellow and brown painting of the aircraft that hangs in his den today, a memento of that great period in his history, gives me shivers. The power of it, the metal, the noise of its lumbering throb down the runway.

Years of late-night war movies clutter my thoughts when I look at that painting, and I try to see my father's young face as one of the frantic, determined men who climbed into those droning planes, their thumbs up at compatriots waiting safe outside on the ground. In all my head-movies, the airmen and soldiers run across tarmac or ruined fields, wearing black-and-white looks of ferocious silence, a look they brought home after the war and incorporated into their patriarchal duties, knowing no other way to be men. And my father — this man I don't know very well — with that same look of ferocity, still on the other side of his glassed-in world.

Foreign Affairs

*A*fter the bombing of her boarding house in Gloucester Terrace, Elizabeth moved to another house on Cromwell Road. The Blitzkrieg continued, though, and it wasn't long before the windows were blown out of the Cromwell Road house. During that same raid, the War Office was severely damaged, destroying many of MI5's secret records, and so the Intelligence office was moved to Blenheim Palace, near Oxford. After the move, Elizabeth commuted up to London to see Dick, the Royal Navy officer she'd been dating. If Elizabeth had stayed in London, I wonder aloud, would she have married the navy boyfriend?

"No, things were coming to an end there anyway."

In the early hours of a 1943 April morning, Elizabeth dozed in the train after an evening of dinner and dancing with Dick, the Navy boyfriend. At Didcot station she was wakened by a commotion outside, and she opened her eyes in sleepy confusion. The passenger sitting opposite rose to peer inquiringly down the corridor but after a moment returned to his seat, shrugging inconclusively at her.

On the platform outside the train, two foreign airmen were attempting to board the Oxford-bound train while it sat in the station. By this time in the war, though, a manpower shortage made it necessary to routinely lock all train carriages after tickets had been collected, preventing non-paying passengers from travelling. The two servicemen moved down the platform, trying the doors of the blacked-out cars without success.

As Elizabeth began to drift into sleep once more, a sudden knocking on the compartment window startled her. Peering through the glass were the two uniformed foreigners, pointing and gesticulating wildly. As the train gave a gentle lurch, Elizabeth's compatriot stood hurriedly, reaching to unlock the window and grab the kit bag shoved at him. The head of a Polish airman materialized through the opening, and Elizabeth watched her fellow passenger haul him in. The Pole landed with a thud and gave a brief smile and a nod before turning to receive the kit bag of the remaining officer, now trotting alongside the moving train. When the second airman also lunged headfirst through the opening, Elizabeth had time only to notice his bright red hair before helping to move the kit bags out of the way.

She wasn't "the sort of girl who would talk to just *any*body," and normally she certainly wouldn't have spoken to two strange men, but it was wartime and these foreigners were fighting for her country.

"I didn't like to be *too* stuffy. After all, this guy had CANADA written all over his shoulder and he looked as if he'd just arrived, fresh off the boat!"

Eric brought out some of the chocolate bars that North American servicemen regularly used on the ration-starved English. The ploy worked on Elizabeth.

"Somehow when I got out at Oxford, I don't quite know how, I'd given him my phone number or something. He'd said, oh, he might come down that way, you know. So off he went and I didn't really think I'd ever hear from him again. But about a month later I got a letter saying he was getting posted to Kidlington, about two miles away from Blenheim Palace, where I was with the War Office."

And the girl who wasn't in the habit of talking to strange men remembered the Canadian airman and the adventure of that midnight train ride. During the intervening month, while Elizabeth had worked six days a week for MI5 counter-intelligence operations, sometimes staying long past midnight to finish urgent dispatches for rapid transit to London HQ and sleeping on a camp bed in an upstairs room of the converted palace, the red-haired Canadian airman had been on all-night flying raids over enemy territory, wondering when — if — he'd see the Pacific Ocean again, the drone of the bomber's engines numbing his thoughts into a kind of trance. And it may have been then, during those dark moments of night thoughts, that the early-morning hours on a train through England's blacked-out countryside took hold of both Eric and Elizabeth, becoming like a kind of dream at the end of a long, sleepless night.

<hr />

"He would come in every time he got a day off and we'd tootle around, floating up and down the river at Oxford and going to movies and going to pubs. Just generally horsing around, you know."

Horsing around? I think, frowning. I calculate their ages quickly: 19 and 20. But this is my mother talking, and I don't want to ask if she did what I did at that age in the dark, at night, with a man.

"So one day I phoned Mother and mentioned that I'd met this Canadian and that I'd like to bring him over for the day or something. And what she said was, 'Well, what can we eat? We haven't got any food.' Because of the rations, you see." Elizabeth rolls her eyes, then shakes her head in exasperation at the memory of my grandmother. "But she came to meet us at the station."

Despite the idiosyncrasies of the inhabitants of Coates Manor, Eric got along "quite nicely" with Granny May. Anthea, though, must have been too rattled by Elizabeth's announcement of an impending visit to be able to relax with the young Canadian.

"The crowning glory was when he took out a cigarette in between courses at lunchtime and lit it!"

"Did they say something to him?"

"No. Granny, to give her her due, was very polite, didn't say a *word*. I would've expected her to expire on the spot, but she didn't say anything at all. I thought, 'Good for you, Granny,' you know? But Mother had that look on her face that said all was not well. That look!"

The look she refers to is full of dark shadows and stewing emotions. It's a look of irrational displeasure and barely concealed anger that instantly changed my grandmother from someone old to something fearsome. The memory of that look strains all our remembrances of Anthea, especially for my mother.

⁓

"She was a pretty frustrated old woman," Eric says of his mother-in-law. He shakes his head slowly, and I understand that this is as close as he can come to appreciating anything about my grandmother. "After *her* break-up, when Elizabeth was only a little, wee pupling, her life must have been terrible. Not a happy one." He thinks about that for a minute, then supplements his explanation: "And of course *her* mother didn't help, you see. Anthea learned that method of dealing with people from Mary Lewton." He considers what he's just said and nods, sure of himself now.

Mary Lewton, though, made a better impression on Eric at that first meeting. The day he came for lunch with Elizabeth's mother and grandmother, Eric thought May was a "lovely old soul."

"I got along with her famously," he remembers, eyes glowing. Then he seems to remember something else and adds as an afterthought, "Even though my table manners weren't the best."

The manor dining room comes to mind, its forever length of table stretching across the marble floors, and I picture my father in his air force blues sitting in the vast hall, chewing contentedly amid the clink of polished silver. Did he even notice the butler and parlour maid standing at attention behind him, the tense silence from my grandmother's place at table or the rebellious surge from Elizabeth's? Was he aware of the colonialism he'd brought into their staid presence? I laugh, discomfited by the thought of his smallness in that house.

"You mean you got along *because* you'd never eaten at that size of table? In that kind of setting?" I ask.

"I guess." He shrugs, flicks the ash from his cigarette, then smiles sheepishly. "I laid my knife and fork down like that." He crosses two pencils to form an X, showing me his faux pas. "You don't *do* that,"

107

he emphasizes, mimicking someone. "Other than that, I got along quite well with the old gal."

"Were *you* overwhelmed by the size of the house?" I ask, remembering its effect on me. That young Canadian serviceman must have been expecting lunch with two old dears in a countryside cottage, seated at a tiny table, perhaps, or in a cramped sitting room. He must have gone expecting to field questions from arthritic and grey-haired widows who spoke in a strange dialect. And maybe, just maybe, he had hoped to be received with some amount of ceremony, to be welcomed as Elizabeth's "young man."

"Oh, I was shocked." His face is long.

"Had Mom given you any indication that she came from that?"

"No! All I knew was to get the train to Kemble and they'd meet me."

"Did they come with the chauffeur?"

"No, no. She had bought this pony with a trap to drive around in during the war. Gas was rationed then, and Mrs. Firth had the Daimler, or whatever it was, up on blocks."

He probably glanced at the large stone gates fronting the long gravel drive to the manor and attributed them to some curious English custom. He might have swallowed in amazement when the pony cart took the long curve and the pillared entrance to the house came into full and glorious view, but then spied the staff cottages beyond the stables and assumed they were headed there.

What must he have told himself when the butler opened the huge oak doors and came down the stairs to greet them?

Knowing my father — knowing myself and how like him I am when unnerved by social situations — he probably began talking to mask his shock.

"Nice house," he might've said. Or, even worse, "Quite the place you got here!"

* * *

After that first visit, Eric never came to the manor again. Bomber Command stepped up the air attack on Hitler, and the young pilot's leaves began to suffer from repeated last-minute cancellations.

He and Elizabeth had already decided to marry, but fearing the repercussions at home over marrying a foreigner, Elizabeth hadn't told her family. After all, Eric was from the colonies, almost an American, and an American was pure anathema to the British upper class — definitely beyond the pale. When Elizabeth finally did tell her mother, Anthea's response was dead silence.

As Elizabeth's 21st birthday approached, Anthea asked her daughter how she'd like to celebrate the occasion. Elizabeth wanted a dinner party in London, but the only place she knew was Claridge's, the "terribly grand and frightfully expensive hotel where Granny May stayed."

Anthea, Elizabeth, Eric and Uncle Phil went out to dinner and then to the theatre, and in the middle of the production, Eric gave Elizabeth an engagement ring.

"When I showed it to Mother at the intermission, I think she nearly threw up. She was horrified!"

"What is he going to *do?*" Anthea worried later to her daughter. "We don't know anything about him or his background."

Anthea, whether on advice from brother Phil or Granny May, wrote off to Dunne and Bradstreet, the international London-based inquiry agency, to find out about the young Canadian and his family. What she discovered was information that Eric had already given Elizabeth, but which had purposely been kept from Anthea.

Eric's father had no bank account whatsoever. He had been bankrupted during the 1930s and was still paying off his debts from mismanaged investments.

"Which, of course, was simply *thrilling* news." My mother grimaces to communicate the messiness of her situation then. "So we didn't make any specific plans about when to get married because we didn't know where 'Ric was going to be sent next, because of all the Air Command turmoil. And then finally, at Christmastime, I think I'd pined away so much and looked so awful that Mother said, 'You might just as well get married if you're going to, you know.' So I phoned him up and we hurriedly arranged the wedding. He was just about to be sent up to Yorkshire, so we had about two weeks' notice."

Family Plot

*E*lizabeth had wanted to include her father, a man she'd met only the year before, at her wedding. But in the end she felt unable to invite him, because if Humphrey had been there, "the world would've come to an end on the spot" for Anthea.

After he and Anthea divorced, Humphrey went to Rhodesia. Elizabeth explains it as a natural emigration: "Like all those other ex-British officers who'd never been trained to do anything except bark commands at people, he went out there and tried to earn a living, growing tea or coffee or whatever they do there." She hesitates. I wait expectantly, and she resumes with a sigh. "But he couldn't even do that properly."

Humphrey met his second wife, a leper missionary, when he was the assistant district commissioner in Tanganyika, 1925-26. When he proposed to her, she went home to England to "think over the engagement" and Humphrey gave up his job to go after her. They returned to Africa to farm tobacco in Southern Rhodesia, where Elizabeth's first half-brother, Christopher, was born in 1927. In later life, Christopher and Elizabeth struck up a fast friendship.

In 1942, Christopher's mother announced in the "Personals" column of *The Times* that Captain L. H. Humphrey Payne was no longer missing, but a POW, and invited his friends to write him. Elizabeth was 21 when she sent the first letter to her estranged father. Humphrey wrote her back from prison camp.

"I showed that letter to my mother because I thought I ought to, and she read it and put it back on my desk and walked out of the room without any comment at all. I never discussed the subject with her again."

Shortly after Humphrey wrote Elizabeth, he was released by the Germans. Considered too frail both emotionally and physically to be of any use to either side, Humphrey was one of those rare prisoners who was freed before the end of World War II. In the fall of 1943, standing under the clock at Victoria Station, Elizabeth met her father for the first time.

"How did you know it was him?" I can't imagine identifying an unknown parent in a crowd of strangers.

"I wandered up toward the clock and I was sort of looking around, you know, and I knew he had the Royal Artillery badge on his hat and I knew his rank — there aren't *too* many officers that stand around under a clock, picking up girls. And, um ... we just sort of both ... I don't know!"

Her grey eyes sparkle and laugh, travel backwards over the years to that day in London. After a morning of anxious fears, spilling coffee on the carefully chosen blouse and riding through the dark Underground wondering who she'd meet at the other end, suddenly he's in front of her, and all the nervous anticipation dissolves in an instant of recognition. Father.

"What did you say, do you remember?" I am under that huge, white-faced clock now, feeling the jostling of anonymous shoulders and arms. Uniforms all around me and I can't tell the difference between a lieutenant and a colonel. I don't even know which is the superior rank. What would I look for?

"No!" Elizabeth tucks her lip beneath her front teeth, shakes her head grimly. I hesitate, wanting to stay in my vision of Victoria Station, but this is her story, not mine, and so I let the picture fade.

"Did you hug him?"

She pauses, thinking. "I don't even remember that ..." And she laughs, startling me. "I don't even remember that. But we went out to lunch and ... oh, it was so funny!"

I sit forward, eager for the dragline that will pull me back into her web of memory.

"It was so like a man, somehow. He'd just come back from this POW camp, and he'd decided he had to go and see his tailor, have a suit made! He had all sorts of extra clothing coupons, I suppose, having been released from the army, and he didn't have much time, he said. You know, he's supposed to be so poor, but he had to go see his tailor and get a new suit made!"

My lip threatens to sneer and I have to fight with it, control the urge to slander and belittle. Like the first Anthea, I'd hoped for a romantic ending, the elusive happily-ever-after scenario. I'd imagined extraordinary words of regret, tears of apology, desperate relief at finding himself cherished after all these years of banishment from his daughter's life. But not this, not another emotional betrayal so thinly disguised. How many chances does a father deserve? How many should a daughter permit?

"We had a pleasant day together, it was quite nice," she burbles, "and then I never saw him again until … he came to see me at Oxford when Eric was missing and I was expecting the baby quite shortly. I guess we must have spoken on the phone or written the odd letter, 'cause he came to see me with the two boys, my half-brothers, and that was the only other time I saw him."

Having spent most of his first wife's and all of his second wife's legacy, even borrowing from his second mother-in-law, Elizabeth's father died a destitute man. Despite all the capital put into the various businesses, each of Humphrey's ventures was eventually foreclosed, and he was forced to declare bankruptcy.

Eric and Elizabeth planned to be married in Oxford. The minister of St. Margaret's Church met with the young couple before the wedding ceremony, as was customary.

"And what hymns shall we have for the service?" He smiled at the bride-to-be, then the groom, inviting their participation.

Eric's eyebrows went up as he pondered the question, then lowered when he smiled in relief at having recalled something. Anything.

"'Abide With Me.'" The hymn he'd heard so many times during his past year in England; the hymn sung at all the service funerals, already played for so many lost friends.

The minister's eyes opened wide, looked questioningly from one to the other of the young couple. He paused as Elizabeth looked down, straightening her skirt, then cleared his throat to speak.

"Well. I don't know if we really want *that* one ..."

Elizabeth suggested "Lead Us, Heavenly Father." She looks at me questioningly. "You know that one?"

I furrow my brow, shake my head quickly and look at my notepad. In that instant I feel as ignorant as my father, as though I should know the hymn, ashamed that I don't.

Elizabeth sings the opening lines for me then, in a high, strained voice that reminds me of old ladies. "*Lead us, heavenly Father, lead us/O'er the world's tempestuous seas.* That's quite a nice cheerful one. We had that and some other one, I guess, and then we went to the Randolph Hotel in the centre of Oxford."

~~~

The night before my mother's wedding, Granny May telephoned to say that Anthea "had this terrible cold and wouldn't be able to come." Elizabeth was both crushed and relieved.

"She'd have been there with a long face anyway, and it wouldn't have been a joyous thing somehow."

So the small wedding party of "20 or so" was mostly Eric's air crew and Elizabeth's few War Office co-workers. Elizabeth's Uncle Phil gave her away, and his wife, Lettice, represented the rest of the family. None of Elizabeth's best friends were invited because they were all in the services and "there wasn't enough time to give them notice. You couldn't just summon up your friends to be bridesmaids because they couldn't get leave anyway."

Elizabeth used all her ration coupons to buy her wedding outfit, a pale blue crêpe dress and wine-coloured hat with a veil. She wore orchids, "which was the fashion then," and an opossum stole — "a fad introduced during the war, and then about six months later all the tarts in London were wearing them too so I never wore mine again!"

She also gave up two weeks of fat and flour rations so that the Randolph Hotel could provide a wedding cake, and the hotel also managed to squeeze a few bottles of champagne out of its cellar.

"I took all this fat and margarine and butter and stuff and they made a *chocolate* cake 'cause they couldn't make a white cake. Couldn't get white icing or something, so they just made a chocolate cake. For our wedding." She sniffs a bit, underlining the indignity of that memory.

And I smile at her patronizingly. Throughout childhood I'd always thought my parents the luckiest couple on the planet to have had chocolate instead of fruit cake at their wedding. But Elizabeth seems to consider that indignity representative of their life together. Always a bit off the mark, not quite quite.

Later, when the sun is sliding in the spring sky and the heavy varnish of the mahogany living-room furniture reflects that dying light, she tells me that when she's in England now, she thinks the English probably wonder who the funny old lady from the colonies is, because she obviously hasn't got the upper-class English accent she used to have. She says it doesn't bother her; it sort of amuses her. She thinks that probably they're not really very interested in her as a person, that maybe it's because she's old and fat with a common name like "Brown."

And when she says that, I cringe with regret for both parents. I remember how I've often made the same comment about my maiden name, how it would hurt my father to hear such blasphemy. His own forefathers — the ones he's tried to trace back to the old world so that he can have a family tree as long and impressive as his wife's — come from another kind of beginning, a different kind of pride and fall.

Below the Salt

*I*n the files my father gives me, I find names I've never heard before. Eric's great-great-grandmother, Jane Hill, comes to New Brunswick on a wooden sailing ship, leaving Ireland and arriving in the new land in 1854. She marries Alexander Atchison of Bathurst, N.B., and has three children. Jane and Alexander's last child, Mary Anne (later Marianne), is born in Newcastle, N.B., where she grows up to marry Fred Weldon in 1889. In 1891, after the birth of my grandmother, Sophie Eileen, Fred and Marianne leave the east coast for Victoria, B.C.

When Eileen is six, her father dies from a fall down the stairs and Eileen is sent back to Newcastle to stay with her aunt. I stop my note-taking to consider this piece of history. How often does someone die from a fall down the stairs? Was Fred pushed, I wonder?

Marianne marries her second husband, William Swinerton, shortly after sending her daughter back east, but nowhere can I find the date of that second wedding. In Eric's research, handwritten notes mention that Swinerton "apparently had money — partner in Swinerton and Addy Real Estate, Victoria." But is that information more reflective of the writer than the subject? Or proof that Marianne's genes were the source of Grandmother Eileen's dark character? Am I being too hard on my Canadian ancestors again?

Eileen returns to Victoria from New Brunswick when she is 18 and, on Wednesday, March 6, 1912, marries Frederick Grant Brown, the boy who lived across the street from her first Victoria home.

The Hills, the Atchisons and the Weldons all seem to descend from the same sort of background as the Firths. Jane Hill was the daughter of a colonel in the British Army, and Alexander Atchison was a respectably wealthy New Brunswick landowner. The Weldons, too, can name British Army officers in their past ranks. But for some reason, none of the family on this side leave anything of material value after their deaths. Their lives are consumed not by the long-term goals of amassing capital like the Firths, but by more day-to-day concerns such as eating, socializing and managing small businesses. When these Canadian relatives die, their wills and testaments list the simpler possessions of life — furniture, property, sentimental items — but no capital, no lists of silver or jewellery, no houses on grand estates.

And when that early branch of Canadian family leaves the conservative east to come to the rough-and-tumble west coast, I discover wives and mothers who raise huge broods of grubby children in the backwoods of B.C.; men who fight for a piece of power in the construction of the newest province, scrapping and drinking with other pioneers who've also come west to make their fortune.

These are my Canadian roots, the source of my restless blood and tough ways.

Fred Grant Brown, the boy Eileen marries, is one of ten children born to Frederick Seymour Brown and Sarah Marie Horne. Fred Seymour, also from the Maritimes, is the 11th child of Nicholas James Brown, an entrepreneur whose shipbuilding business flourishes during the reciprocity agreements of the American Civil War, but afterwards fails, putting Fred Seymour's dad into deep debt and the possibility of debtors' prison.

When his father's troubles peak, therefore, Fred Seymour decides to make his own way in life. He leaves the family home in Port Hastings, Cape Breton Island, and makes his way across the continent. He arrives in Victoria sometime during the early 1880s, still less than 20 years of age.

The city of Victoria has been in existence for only about 30 years at the time of Fred Seymour's arrival. In 1883, after Victoria had been the capital city of the new Province of British Columbia for some 12 years, the federal government under Macdonald offered acreage on southeastern Vancouver Island and a grant of $750,000 to Robert Dunsmuir, owner of a large Nanaimo coal mine, to build the Esquimalt & Nanaimo Railroad. By 1884, Fred Seymour finds work as the first telegraph operator and train dispatcher for the new E&N Railroad.

In July of 1885, Frederick Seymour Brown marries Sarah Marie Horne, daughter of Adam Grant Horne ("First white man to cross Vancouver Island") and Sarah Marie (née Bates), the "full-blooded redskin" about whom my father has previously boasted but who is actually, I later discover, the sister of English immigrant Mark Bates, first mayor of Nanaimo. After their marriage, Fred and Sarah move to Yale, B.C., where Fred is hired as postmaster and operator of the Government Telegraph Office. Eventually Fred Seymour and Sarah Marie settle north of Nanaimo in the small village of Union Bay, where Fred becomes the first postmaster. Together they raise ten children; Fred Grant, Eric's father, is the third.

Fred Seymour sounds remarkably similar in tone to my father, his grandson. In various memoirs, comments about Fred's boorish attitude are strikingly familiar: "As a kid, when you went into the post office, Mr. Brown would ask, 'What the hell are you doing in here?'" Or, "Dad went to bed every night at 9:00 PM. He wouldn't give a darn who was there — the mayor, the king of England. He just said good night, poured his bath for the morning and went to bed." Rough people living in rough times.

I read all this information in my father's file, and what seems most notable is the repetition of the men's Christian names. I wonder if having three Freds in as many generations is reflective of the lower social status of my Canadian family or if Fred in those days was as plain a name as John seems now.

Eric's father always seemed rather fine to me, his white hair neatly oiled and combed and his strong, fresh scent — lavender water? — lingering after a hug. I remember his pink-shaven cheeks, jowly and smooth in contrast to my father's coarse beard, and there was also something dapper about this man, the only grandfather I ever knew.

Maybe it was the smart crease in the brim of his fedoras or the forward tilt at which he wore them. And when he took his suit jacket off, the metal spandex armbands that kept his shirt cuffs from sliding past his slender wrists made him seem important, businesslike. I think he wore sock garters too, though that's just a vague memory, and I'm not sure now how I could have known such a thing because they would never have been seen, would have been considered as intimate as underwear.

But then I think how there are always certain attributes missed by a grandchild reminiscing about a dead grandparent, and perhaps this is why I never saw the darker side that others always mentioned about my granddad Fred.

Even before he died, there were bitter stories whispered about Fred's brutishness. How he didn't give a damn about anyone but himself, never paid his bills, shoved them in a drawer where Rose, my step-grandmother, would find them months later. Or he'd ask for fresh asparagus in the middle of winter, and when his wife glanced knowingly at my mother, Elizabeth would shake her head. But then Rose would get up and write "asparagus" on her shopping list, just as Fred wanted. And later my mother would explain that asparagus cost three times the price of any other vegetable in winter and that Rose and Fred had only their old-age pensions to live off, but Rose always did what Fred ordered. Like Eileen, his first wife, my grandfather Fred was not always easily loved.

And yet Fred was the person who took in my brother during some hard years of Chris' adolescent crises, no small gesture for such an old man. Fred would have been well on in years by then — perhaps seventy-five or -six — and though giving Chris a home did not seem to help my brother, it did reveal a soft streak in the rough side of the family.

A Matter of Time

*W*as my mother smitten by romantic notions of her Canadian airman? Was she, like many Brits, convinced that a North American background somehow equated to a rough-and-ready, pioneer mentality? Was she taken by the idea that Eric's trailblazing forefathers meant he was made of the same stuff?

For their honeymoon, Eric and Elizabeth spent four short nights on the Cornish seaside at Torquay. It was January 1944, and the British war machine was building for an upcoming offensive. Leave, when granted at all, was extremely limited, and newlyweds were lucky to have a honeymoon of any kind.

Right after the honeymoon, Eric was posted to Skipton in Yorkshire. Elizabeth was not allowed to go with him, restricted by the requirements of her National Services job.

She worked six days out of seven and only had a weekend off "maybe once a month."

"Did you do that without grumbling?" I ask with baby-boomer incredulity.

And her stock response, so foreign to my generation: "Well, there was work to be done for the nation, you know. Nobody questioned it. If there was something that had to be finished, we sometimes stayed and worked until midnight."

"Did you get extra pay for it, at least?"

"Oh dear, no!" she laughs at me. "Nothing like that! Got three pounds a week."

I'm momentarily shocked. I do some mental calculations. "Was that good pay? Or just normal?"

"It was pretty poor. They were mostly people who, I guess, had some private money and didn't really need their salaries all that much anyway, the ones that were working there."

"But," I blubber, "you needed that money. I mean, you weren't getting an allowance from your mother?"

Elizabeth shakes her head, eyes wide open, forehead lifted in waves of wrinkles. "She used to send me a cheque every three months or so. I didn't have much left after I paid my rent; I had very little to go out for an occasional meal or something."

"Didn't it ever occur to you to talk to your mother about an allowance, like she had when she was your age?"

"No!" Elizabeth coughs out a grim sort of laugh. "It just wasn't done."

"So ..." I hesitate, confused. "How did you and Dad plan on supporting yourselves while ... I mean, did he get a decent paycheque from the air force?"

"Oh, I don't know!" Elizabeth smiles gaily, waving her hand as she sits back against the couch, laughing at such trivial details.

I frown, totally abashed. "You didn't think about things like that?"

"No, no!" She looks at me daringly. "Terrible, wasn't it!" And then she tilts her head, considers. "Well, he got quite good pay, I suppose. About 40 pounds a month as a pilot officer."

"Was *that* a lot?"

"No." Laughing. "But we were young and healthy and we didn't think about things like that. There was never any question about things like unemployment in those days."

"What about birth control, Mom? Did you think about that?" Another question I've been wanting to ask for some 30-odd years. Reading about the rampant spread of VD and gonorrhea during the war, I've learned how the allied soldiers in particular were issued condoms as stock supplies. But I've never asked my mother about this important consideration in her life before today.

And she doesn't miss a beat. "Oh yes, I went to the doctor before getting married and got fitted up for a cap — a cervical cap, not the normal diaphragm thing. But I must've put it in all ass-backwards because … well, you know, I got married on January the 15th and about two weeks later I started feeling sick." She grimaces, makes a funny face and adds, "Ha, ha," only semi-humorously.

"Really. That fast."

"Just like that."

"Boom. Wow."

The intelligent conversation of two women remembering the oscillating feelings of a first pregnancy.

I wait a moment before asking, "Was he pleased when he found out you were pregnant? Or was he scared silly?"

"No, I think he was quite pleased. Oh yeah." She nods, definite about this memory.

"Were you?" I hold my breath.

"Yes, I was too, actually. I mean, I might as well be doing that as anything else, and a lot of other people had the same attitude, I think. You never knew if your partner was going to get killed the next day, so if you were going to reproduce, you might as well get on with it."

"Weren't you scared to think that he might die, though, and you'd be stuck all alone with this kid?" The projections of a single parent, comparing the dark ages of contemporary society to the even darker ages of an earlier society.

She shrugs. "Yes, but … In a sort of way I didn't even stop to think about it." She looks right at me, her crow's feet wrinkling with the softness of a slight smile. "It's weird, isn't it?"

I shake my head. "It's incredible." And then another thought occurs to me. "Have you ever thought about what your mother would have done? I mean, would she have taken you in, complaining bitterly about this child that was hanging around?"

The answer is quick and neat. "I doubt it."

And just as instantly I feel bad for putting my grandmother in a punishable position again.

Elizabeth was five or six months pregnant, the time when female employees were allowed to leave their essential-services jobs, when Eric was shot down over France. The telegram announcing his MIA status was sent to Coates Manor, where Anthea, not wanting to tell Elizabeth herself, phoned her daughter's roommate.

"Stella sat me down to tell me. She sat me down and read out the telegram message."

"Do you remember what it said?"

"'The Department of National Defence regrets to inform you that your husband Flying Officer Eric Brown is reported missing in action.'" Memorized words spoken in officialese.

"What did you do?" I want to access a specific moment, her feelings and reactions to the telegram.

But perhaps Elizabeth doesn't understand the question. She begins to relate her subsequent actions.

She phoned the Air Ministry to find out what had happened, whether his plane had been shot down in flames or simply disappeared on the way back to base.

"But the officials there couldn't — or wouldn't — give me any information."

She phoned the Yorkshire base where the lumbering Halifax had last been seen lifting up into the 1944 June night. Eric's squadron leader was "very nice," but also unable to tell her anything.

For six weeks she wandered in a daze, numbed by thoughts of her future gone awry. And in that peculiar manner of remembering something from long ago, her memory dredged up an old prediction. Early in the war, a fortuneteller had told Elizabeth that her husband would die in the service of the Crown. Being an unmarried girl without any prospects of marriage at the time, she'd forgotten the prediction as soon as it was given. But when the bad news arrived, Elizabeth became consumed with the fatalistic idea that she'd always known, or should have known, Eric wouldn't be a permanent part of her life.

By then the invasion of Normandy was on and "the world was upside down. We all lived from day to day in a state of paralysis during that time. I remember thinking he might come back or he might not, but there wasn't a thing I could do about it except try and stay healthy for the baby."

Elizabeth was getting big. The baby was due in another month, and so she occupied her time with preparations for bringing Baby home. One afternoon, after shopping for clothes and other infant paraphernalia, Elizabeth stood at the door of the Oxford cottage shared with Stella, another war bride, struggling to fit the key into the lock while balancing her parcels. The mail on the floor inside jammed the door as she pushed against it, and Elizabeth put her bundles down in order to reach in and free the blockage. When the door swung freely, the pile of mail scattered, but one piece, a clearly marked envelope, caught her eye: *Kriegsgefangenepost.* Prisoner of War mail. Elizabeth's name and address, in Eric's handwriting, glared up at her from the envelope.

The Red Cross was the usual channel of notification when a missing serviceman was taken POW, but Elizabeth had heard nothing from them. Ten days later, after a second letter had arrived, Elizabeth phoned the Red Cross to tell them about the correspondence she'd received and to ask for confirmation of her husband's whereabouts. They knew nothing about Eric's POW status but wanted to follow up her information. They asked her to surrender the two letters she'd received.

Elizabeth wrote to Eric at the address on the back of his letters and then she notified his parents, Fred and Eileen, in Vancouver. Eileen immediately packed up some parcels of food and cigarettes, sending them via the Red Cross, but Eric never received anything.

"That was a particularly crucial stage in the war when none of the mail was getting anywhere," Elizabeth explains. "A total mess. There was a sort of last-ditch effort by the Germans, I guess, and everything was concentrated on winning."

Then, before any officials, air force or Red Cross, had contacted her about Eric's location, Elizabeth received a phone call from him. Less than a month had passed since she'd discovered he was still alive. The English summer had been long and hot, and when the phone rang that night Elizabeth was still awake, her expanded girth adding to her sleeplessness in the uncomfortable heat.

"Hello, darling." The voice was weak but unmistakably familiar. Eric, calling from an American hospital in Somerset where he'd been taken, barely alive, by the American troops.

I look at the picture Elizabeth shows me of her young husband just back from the POW camp in Rheims, bone-thin and gaunt. The once-thick mop of red hair is gone.

"When I went to see him in hospital, I walked right by him, looking up and down the ward for this red hair." She pauses, bites her lip. "It was almost white and ... very sparse. He'd aged quite a bit."

"How long was he a POW?" I ask, meaning "How long did it take to get this skinny, this worn down?"

"Two months. Two and a half months. From the end of June 'til early September."

"So it wasn't just being in the POW camp that did this to him. It was being in the hospital and fighting for his health too?"

"I guess, yes. They got very little food and terribly little medication. I think that just the pain and total upset of the whole thing, as well as the diet, was what did it in the end."

We're both still staring at the black-and-white photo of my pyjama-clad father on crutches, and I'm unsure of the "it" my mother refers to, but I don't ask. This is the first photo taken after my father lost his right leg, and my subconscious is doing funny things, trying to shut down, I think, because I find myself wondering about the possibility of a fuzzy connection between dangling and misplaced modifiers and dangling and misplaced limbs.

"This" — I point to the skeletal figure in the photo — "is from a lack of nutrition, then?"

"Just shock, I think. Shock and pain and everything."

End of the Day

My father the war veteran has always been a source of ambivalence for me. Hero or martyr, I'm never really sure how to accept him.

I listen to his level voice telling me how his Halifax bomber was shelled during a night raid over Rheims and how, when he looked down at his right leg, he couldn't find his foot. I ask him if that hurt and he looks surprised, shakes his head, says no and continues talking, telling me how he had to make sure his crew was evacuated before jumping himself, how he hit his now-dangling leg on the rudder while trying to escape the diving plane, blacking out as he fell through the popping French sky.

He regained consciousness in a French farmer's field, opening his eyes to the faces of a dog and a young man bending over him, and though he badly needed a drink of water, his minimal knowledge of French prevented him from remembering the word. Later they transported him on what he thinks must have been a wagon, taking him into their home and keeping him in the cellar, trying to help. Twenty-four hours later, he says, the French family realized he would die without medical intervention. They called in the Gestapo, who moved Eric to the Rheims POW hospital.

I shudder when my mother insists the leg might have been saved if the Nazis hadn't denied him proper medical care. In the POW camp, they allowed the infection to fester until the leg needed to be amputated.

Elizabeth's eyes narrow as she describes how the German doctors sharpened the amputation knife in front of my gangrene-ridden father. My mother, probably out of loyalty to her husband and patriotic hatred of the Nazis, has repeated this story for years. There was no anaesthetic available — or, at least, none given to POWs. And when the camp was liberated by Patton's forces and Eric was shipped back to England, the shock of red hair he'd taken overseas had paled beyond the possibility of even calling it sandy, thinned so completely that henceforth he would be described as balding. The English physicians pronounced the amputation poorly done and began a series of orthopaedic surgeries intended to make the best of a bad situation.

When I was young and impressionable, I believed in the evilmindedness of all Germans and wore my school poppy on Remembrance Day with more than a little disdain for the other children in my class whose fathers had stayed home, avoiding the war and the fight for justice. I grew up with my father's limp as a constant reminder of what he'd lived through for the rest of the democratic world, but always, always I felt a sense of doubt behind the mixture of pride and embarrassment for my one-legged father.

By the time I was 13 or 14, the hand-washed stump socks drying on the bathroom towels were something I didn't notice except when a new friend asked about the oversized condoms hanging there. My father built a pool, and my mother suggested it was so he could swim somewhere without people staring or making rude comments about his public display of an incomplete anatomy. It never occurred to me that I should shoo my friends out of the backyard so he could have his swim in privacy, even when I'd see them trying to look at his stump without being noticed. He'd emerge from the change room on crutches, dropping them when he reached the diving board and crawling out to the end, flinging himself forward with the weight of his arms alone.

He swam with his eyes scrunched up, though one of them is nearly blind. And when he turned his head to take a breath, his lips pursed forward like a codfish, sucking at the air like an oxygen pump. But he had powerful arms that made his front crawl seem effortless, and you couldn't tell when he was moving through the chlorinated blue of the water that he was not a whole man.

Whenever the Department of Veterans' Affairs provided him with a new leg, the old one would be stored in case of emergency. He keeps the oldest one at his favourite lakeside retreat near 100 Mile House, and once when I was trying to impress a new boyfriend with my wilderness skills, we went together to this northern waterfront that my father had taught me to love. It was a long hot drive through the Fraser Canyon and into the Cariboo and we arrived ready to jump in the lake. I unlocked the bath-cum-cookhouse built sometime in the early '60s, and the new boyfriend went in to change.

"Jesus Christ!" he yelled from behind the closed door.

"What? What's wrong?" I called from outside, hand reaching for the knob.

When he opened the door again, he was pale with fright, pointing at something. I crooked my head around the barricade between us and saw, leaning against the wall, my father's spare leg, flesh-coloured plastic with stainless-steel joints and linen straps. The flush of an unnameable emotion was instant, and I sneered, "It's only my father's leg, you idiot. What did you think it was?"

When the Vietnam crisis exploded and American draft dodgers flooded the sidewalks of Vancouver's Fourth Avenue, it was a revelation to discover that Eric's veteran status might be a disgrace. Previously my father had been some kind of saviour, donating life and limb to the destruction of the Nazi machine, but recent protests about the unnecessary cruelties of war began to fill me with shame for his service record. I asked him if he would go to war again were he an 18-year-old American facing the draft, and his response convinced me of his apparent ignorance.

"Goddamned right!" he assured me, blue eyes blazing.

Knowing what he'd lived through during World War II — the utter devastation of his 21-year-old youth — and knowing the extreme war tactics of the Nixon government, I could make no sense of his answer.

For years I'd heard Eric and Elizabeth belittle the Americans for staying out of World War II until the last minute, by which time all other Allied forces were so depleted that U.S. intervention allowed the Americans to claim they'd stopped the Germans and ended the war. So when the nightly news coverage began to show visual footage of the U.S. napalm attacks on remote Vietnamese villages, I equated my father's assurances of re-enlistment with support for this blatant devastation of life. How could I believe in his heroism then?

The Vietnam experience taught my generation that a government's military tactics can fuel extreme patriotism with dangerous results. So in the 1960s, in the interests of international peace and out of a love for my misguided father, I honoured all war heroes in the way I knew best. I smoked marijuana, wore long hair and dresses with beads, spent time at peace marches, protests and be-ins, and rejected all trust in the infallibility of democracy. I believed my father was right to discredit the 1945 fable of American superiority but didn't understand why he couldn't recognize the resurrection of that same pompous attitude in Vietnam. I stopped acknowledging my father's bravery and started criticizing his foolishness for going off to war, a young and ignorant boy who thought he could make the world a better place by fighting.

But that same father, though he'd never admit to having made what I consider a mistake, has shown me the value of personal conviction. Still, it is not until a day years later, when I hear another version of that night over Rheims, that I begin to understand the merit in the younger Eric's decisions.

My father keeps in touch with one of the remaining two air crew still alive. Ralph, the bomber's navigator, has Alzheimer's, so it is only Howard, the tail gunner, who can relate his memories of that long, dark night.

⌒

In 1995, when Howard and his wife come to B.C., Eric and Elizabeth bring them to visit me on the Sunshine Coast. I've met Howard before, at the 25th anniversary of the end of the war, but it is not until the 50th anniversary that I begin to appreciate the connection between my father and this man. On a windy August afternoon, sitting beside the roar of Georgia Strait, I ask Howard what he remembers of the young pilot Eric Brown.

Despite his senior years, Howard is a big man. He looks away from me when I ask the question, stares across the Strait at the billowing smoke of the Harmac pulp mill south of Nanaimo before answering. I wait, wondering if maybe I shouldn't have asked him such a question, if maybe he can't remember too much anymore. And then he speaks, clearing his throat softly first. "No one else could bring a bomber in like Eric," he tells me. He lifts his right hand, the free one, the other one holding a beer can, and planes his palm, face down, toward his lap, in imitation of those remembered smooth landings. "Half the time you couldn't tell whether the plane had touched down or if it was still in the air." He shakes his head before he looks back at me. "It was somethin' else."

What about the man himself, I want to know. What was that 20-year-old like?

"He was a brash sonofabitch. He'd watch another pilot bring a plane in, then go out and tell him what he'd done wrong. He didn't worry about their feelings — he just wanted things done right. It gave us a lot of confidence to know he was like that."

I smile at the poignant observation, recognizing that I would have missed this noteworthy fact about my father were it not for Howard. I wait a few more moments, then ask about the night they were shot down. What does Howard the tail gunner remember of that, I want to know?

Howard puts down his beer can and lifts his hands once more, showing me what happened that night. He holds one hand horizontal — the Halifax — and tilts the other one underneath. The second hand — the enemy fighter — is aimed at the soft underbelly of the palm above it.

"This fighter pilot was shooting at the front end of the plane, where your dad was," he explains, "and then he came back towards me at the rear of the plane. His plane was still tilted up, like this" —

Howard shakes the inclined hand to emphasize the fighter's position beneath the bomber — "aiming at us. And I shot at him."

"Did you get it?" I ask.

"Oh, yeah!" he snorts. "I took care of the bastard, all right."

Later, when my father takes a nap and Howard goes for a walk, I lie in the hammock intending to read, but the sound of the crashing waves against the August heat lulls me into a doze, and I drift through visions of a night sky lit by the flames of fighters and explosions from ground artillery. The flares slip past the window of the airplane around me until a sudden fireball hurls us into the rushing whine of descent, our speed increasing while the altitude drops. And when I wake with a jolt, the blue sky screams in my eyes.

I turn my head dazedly, see Howard standing at the edge of the Strait staring out at the distance beyond. I look at his profile and can only imagine the tight connection between the young men on that bomber and these old men here today. Their interdependence on — their pride in — each other's skills. The sigh of relief, unheard, that must have gone up each time the lumbering Halifax touched down at Skipton after a long night lost in enemy skies.

Out of Darkness

*E*ric gives me his Pilot's Flying Log Book and I turn to the last few pages of entries. I am surprised to find that he only flew two months of bombing missions before being shot down. Some of the names of the targets are familiar.

April 24, Karlsruhr

April 30, Somaine — very clear — light flak, no searchlights

May 20, Mined the Kattegatte — nothing seen, no flak

May 22, bombed Le Mans — target well lit, light flak, 9000'

May 24, bombed Aachen — heavy flak, attacked 4x by night fighters, target wiped out, 17,500'

June 5, D Day — bombed Houlgate gun emplacement — 12000' — 8000 lbs; attack by one night fighter

June 6, bombed Conde-sur-Noireau — road junction — 4000' — 8000 lbs

June 9, bombed airfield of Le Mans — 2000' — 8000 lbs — 3 search lights — moderate light flak — target well lit

June 12, bombed Arras — coned by searchlights — lost an engine — 5800' — 8000 lbs — late on return

June 14, bombed Cambrai — 18,800' 8000 lbs — heavy flak guns — marshalling yards well pranged

June 15, Daylight to Boulogne — 8000 lbs — 15,500' — heavy flak — Spitfire screen

The red line under the last entry is final:

June 28, Metz — missing

He tells me about the experience of flying over enemy territory in the dark, with 500-pound bombs (H2s, fully operational) lying behind him in the body of the Halifax Mark III. I am acutely aware as I listen that this is an experience I will never have.

"Joining up was a lot of fun until you smelled cordite," he says.

"Smelled what?"

"Cordite. The smell of fumes from a bullet. If you can smell cordite, you know you're not going to get hit. If you don't smell the cordite, look out."

"So the first time you smelled cordite, did you realize something was changing in your life?"

"I realized there was somebody trying to kill me. I didn't like that." He chuckles as if he's said something funny. "We thought, 'Christ, this is for real! They're trying to kill us!' "

"Did it become personal then?"

"I don't know about personal. I mean, it was kill or be killed. Whenever we went up, we all knew that we could be killed in a matter of seconds."

"So before you went up, were your goodbyes —"

His interruption is emphatic. "We never said goodbye." He shakes his head but doesn't look at me or offer an explanation.

"What'd you say?" It's like pulling teeth from a wild boar, trying to draw information from this man.

"We always said, 'See you tomorrow.' "

"With the thought in the back of your mind that maybe you wouldn't, or … ?"

"You couldn't think of that. You never *dared* think of that." He pauses, a long, arduous pause, and I squirm with the tension of waiting. "You knew damned well you may not come back, but it was … just silly."

I look at him quizzically, but he is looking at his shoes. He starts to continue and this time it is me who interrupts.

"Silly?" Trying to keep the doubt out of my voice.

"Yeah. Silly."

"That makes it sound almost humorous."

"Well, it was humorous. If you're going to take off with a bomb load and say to yourself, 'Christ, I may never come back,' you're being sombre and you probably won't." He laughs again, a heavy, throaty laugh, and I can't tell whose benefit it's for.

This is the tone of so many of my conversations with this man who is my father. A man who doesn't want to be uncovered, a man so wary that when we approach him with love — or the closest thing to love that any of us can handle, usually respect, sometimes fear — he turns away. I have no idea how to interpret his punctuating laugh.

"Okay," I say slowly, groping for another way into the mine of his memories. "In that light, then, did you ever get up there and think, 'What the hell am I doing here? This is bloody ridiculous! Why don't I just jump ship and go home?'" I hear myself use the words "bloody" and "hell" and am surprised at how foreign they sound, coming from me. For a brief moment I wonder if I used those words in order to identify with him. Or maybe so that he would identify with me.

He gives me an indecipherable look, a slight smile around his mouth but his eyes a world away. A soft snicker escapes before he shakes his head.

"Never. No. You never thought that. You were fearful ..." He stops, changes his mind, looks out the window and starts again. "You weren't fearful leaving or coming home. Fear started to set in, in its funny little way, as soon as you crossed the enemy coast. You may not have seen anything, going over an enemy port, but you knew you were crossing over their territory."

"And you could get shot down any minute."

He chuckles again, then carefully rephrases my explanation. "You knew that there were guys down there trying to kill you."

It's an important differentiation, to him. My version is fatalistic: "could get shot down any minute" implies an inevitability delayed only by time or fate, factors beyond human control. His version — "there were guys down there trying to kill you" — suggests that death was within his personal power to avoid. And maybe it was. Maybe one day I'll get the words right enough that he won't need to correct me.

"When the shell came through your fuselage that day —" I stop, unprepared for the emotion surging up my back and grabbing at my throat. I swallow, jump in again. "Were you prepared for that? Did it happen without any warning?"

"It just happened."

"Did you know what had happened? When you saw it, did your mind grasp the meaning of it?" This is the moment I have wanted to know about all my life.

"All I knew," his voice rises above mine, drowns the end of my question, "was that my starboard inner engine was on fire." He enunciates each word very precisely, the way I remember his voice on the dictaphone the year I was 16, working for a summer at his law firm. He always spoke carefully into the microphone when recording notes from a file, preparing for a trial. Meticulous words picked specifically, purposefully, like bits of lint from a dark suit.

"You could see the flames." I say it as if to confirm the picture I've drawn from his words.

"Oh, Christ yeah. They were all over the bloody place."

"What went through your head?" Beneath the sternum a huge pressure is building as I hold my breath, waiting for the interest on that million-dollar question.

"I thought, 'How the hell did that happen?' I mean, I didn't see any bullets or any other damned thing. It was my engineer who said, 'Skipper, your engine's on fire.' I looked out and by God it is." I hear the present tense and watch him closely, see something in his eyes flickering back and forth between that night sky of 1944 and this grey room in April some 50 years later. When his voice stops, I sit tensely, unmoving and silent, waiting. After a few seconds, afraid of losing him to the blackness of memories, I urge him on.

"What happened then?" I ask softly. "What did you think?"

"Well, I figured ..." His brow folds into frown lines as his voice fades a moment. "A ... Maybe an oil line had broken or something. I didn't see any bullets." He shakes his head, caught in that moment of disbelief once again. I wait some more. "So I feathered the engine — put the propeller in direct line with the wind so it won't turn around — and it wouldn't feather properly. And I put the fire extinguisher on, a little button over here" — he moves his hand across an imaginary dashboard and I stare, fascinated, at those swollen and gnarled fingers flicking the switch — "and the fire wouldn't go out because every time the propeller turned around, a flame appeared. And I was cursing. This goddamned propeller ... not feathering itself." His speech is slowing noticeably, interspersed with great gashes of silence, flashes of memory. "And then bang! The dashboard went out. I didn't realize I'd been hit."

"You didn't feel that?" The words are a surprise to me. The question slips out despite my not wanting to interrupt, and I am relieved when he is not distracted by it.

"No, I didn't feel a thing. Didn't see where it came from. It obviously came from over ... somewhere behind my right shoulder. Didn't hit my engineer, who was right behind me. Hit me in my leg. Hit me in the face. *That* I felt." He winces slightly, but not, I think, in memory of the physical pain. Just the work of uncovering, remembering, drilling through so much darkness. "And so ... I told the crew to bail out. And uh ... the fellows at the back got out. The ones in the front got out. My navigator came up to the front to see how I was, to open the hatch. And I couldn't ... walk. I couldn't get up." He looks right at me then, his blue eyes open wide like a small child filled with wonder.

I don't know if he widens them in order to try and see me better — the explosion over France that night legally blinded one eye and the other is blinding from old age — or if he wants to assure himself of where he is while reliving that terrifying flash of memory. Even the pouches and pockets of loose skin and dark shadows don't detract from the sudden surprise I see in his eyes now.

"That was the first time you realized you'd been hit in your leg?"

"Yeah." He looks away again. "So fortunately my engineer hadn't left. Or maybe he had but he turned around and came back again, I don't know. Anyway, he asked me what was wrong. Why wasn't I getting out? I told him, 'I can't *walk* ... ' So he put ... what we call a chest harness on me. A parachute. Took the straps off my back which had the seat harness ... opened the dinghy hatch above my head and ... helped me go out there ..." His voice is weakening, disappearing into the thick air of emotion in this room, the noise of the tape recorder whirring away in the background. I fill the silence, so he won't stop, won't bog down in the feelings he can't talk about but which flood through him now.

"He heaved you out ..."

He nods at the wall. "Next thing I remember was ... the parachute opening. I don't recall pulling the cord, but I guess I must have. And, when the parachute opened, I lost the flying boot off the leg that had been shot. It disappeared. I remember looking at my sock and thinking, 'What the hell?' I still wasn't having any pain. I knew that I was hit, though, because I couldn't walk."

My mother has told me another story about that night over France. As he fell through the night sky, drifting in and out of consciousness, Eric heard a voice. An old friend from his Vancouver school days, another boy who'd gone overseas with him, speaking with strong words of reassurance.

"You're going to be all right, Brownie," the voice said. "You're going to be all right."

Elizabeth has warned me that Eric probably won't tell me this part of the story. He doesn't like to talk about it, she says, because he can't explain it. Barrie, whose voice he'd heard, was killed in France, but it was another six months before Eric learned of his friend's death. What spooked him was the official record of Barrie's MIA status: June 6, long before Eric's last mission.

I sit in tense anticipation, waiting for the story about the voice in the sky. But I am disappointed almost immediately.

"And then I saw ... I thought that ... I saw what appeared to be a cloud layer. And I thought, 'Well, I must have bailed out at about 18,000 feet so I've still got a long way to go.' What that cloud layer was was just fog on the ground. So I was quite totally relaxed when I hit the ground."

I am falling through the black night sky with him, lost in the confusion of fog and surreal memories. It's such a powerfully real moment that I'm afraid of getting lost here, back in his memory. I want to come back to my own body so I insist, somewhat sternly, "You must have felt *that* on your leg," and he finishes the thought for me.

"Yeah, I did." He laughs again, though not quite so convincingly any more, and I wonder about taking a break, leaving this place in his past for something more present, but before I can suggest it, he begins again. I watch his hands, alive now, moving descriptively in the air instead of holding his beer can protectively. "Anyway, I thought, 'So be it. I'm here, I can't walk.' I tried, actually, to get up. Thought, 'Maybe this isn't that bad,' but I couldn't. So I pulled the parachute in and retired it."

"Retired" leaps out, tweaks my editing senses. Wrong word, I think, before remembering his meticulousness. So does he choose it because of his background in law and a need for accuracy, or is this an actual term used by airmen to describe the pulling-in of a used parachute? I am aware, as I focus on his choice of words, that my protectiveness, my feelings of guilt about dragging him back to this buried memory are making it difficult to stay in the moment of the story with him. This painful flight back, so distracting, so hard for me to hear that I will choose almost anything else to worry about rather than the emotions at hand.

I force myself to refocus. "Was that to let people know where you were?"

"Sure!"

"Or were you trying to hide?"

"Oh no — I wasn't going to hide anywhere!" He laughs, another overly loud punctuation in the conversation and a subtle ridicule of my Hollywood knowledge of what goes on in a war. In that instant, I'm a child again, confused by his light dismissal of a real question. When he resumes, I pay closer attention, coming back to the story in time to see him frowning, sinking into concentration. "So I retire the parachute," he says, "and then about … what seemed five minutes or so, I heard a dog barking and I guess about … I don't know how long. I must have passed out." His voice drifts away from me, becomes almost a mumble. "Next thing I knew I was … there was a bunch of French people around. And they put me onto a wagon. And I must have passed out again because I woke up downstairs in the basement of this farmhouse."

"They were hiding you?"

"Mm-hmm."

"Was there somebody down there with you or did they just put you in a bed and close up the cellar?"

"Oh no. There was a couple of Frenchmen and a couple of ladies. And eventually" — I lean forward to hear, his voice weakening still further — "a French lady with a red cross around her arm. And she told me … I'm going to have to go to hospital, otherwise I'm going to die. Because the leg injury and loss of blood was such that … they had no other choice."

"This was all in French?"

"Some. The girl with the red cross could speak a little English." He squints at me, trying to remember something else. "I couldn't remember the French word, *l'eau*. They kept feeding me wine, but every time I drank the wine, I threw up." We both laugh, me loudest, a shallow acknowledgment of the horror and the fear.

When he continues, I hear in his pacing that the story is becoming a struggle now. "Anyway, the next day they got … the Gestapo and … they took me off to hospital. And they were very kind, the Gestapo. Treated me like a little baby." I wait, almost a full minute of sharp silence, for him to continue. "And that was the end of that," he announces with sudden resumption of volume, looking directly at me. I sit back with a jerk, surprised.

"But when … I thought …" I fumble with the words, totally confused. Start again. "I've always heard horror stories, I guess from Mom, about how they actually *took* the leg off. That wasn't the Gestapo, then?" I ask.

"Oh, that was the hospital people." His chair creaks as he shifts himself, his half-leg tucking itself beneath the whole one, as if it were trying to hide from us, and then his tone changes and he seems annoyed. "Not a horror story at all. There was nothing horrible about it. I choose to believe that they didn't have any anaesthetic. Maybe they did — I don't know."

"These are Germans, not Frenchmen."

"Well, a French doctor took my leg off, a French surgeon. A German doctor was in charge of me, but it was a French doctor who took my leg off."

"So were you actually in a POW camp at this time, or was the hospital separate?"

"Yeah — it was a POW hospital."

"And you never saw any of your crew again in that POW camp?"

"Oh no, I did!" The question, or maybe the memory, animates him, and he is energized again. "My mid-upper gunner was in the same cell as me. And, though I didn't know it, my tail gunner was about ... five, six cells down. He knew *I* was there, but I didn't know *he* was there."

"And were you actually in cells with bars on the door?"

"Oh yeah."

"I somehow imagined you were in rooms like ... you know, in *King Rat*? That movie?"

"Oh no, no, no. We were in cells about the size of this room with an iron door, or bars on the door, and a little window up here with iron bars there, and the windows all looked on the compound down below."

"And the walls were all concrete, I guess."

"No. It was brick, red brick. And down in the compound we were patrolled by a Doberman pinscher."

"Did they let you out in the yard once in a while? Oh, but I guess you couldn't walk anyway ..."

"No, no. They took us out, those who had amputations. They took us out once a week. If the weather was nice. But they didn't take the other prisoners out, the ones who didn't have amputations."

"They were worried about them trying to escape?"

"I guess so."

"So you just sat in the yard?"

"They put you ... individually. About ten feet away from each other."

"You weren't allowed to talk?"

He shakes his head for a long time, like a pendulum winding down.

"How many people were in the camp?"

He tilts his neck, computes silently for a long pause. "Had to be ... 1,500."

Then he tells me, twice, like a tour guide dropping a morsel of triviality at my feet, that the Rheims Memorial Hospital was built by the United States government after the First World War. He repeats this information as if he's trying to remember something, and I wait for him to elaborate on the detail, but nothing is forthcoming.

"What did you do in there every day?" I ask eventually.

"Nothing."

"You must have thought!"

"Oh, you did a lot of thinking."

"What did you think about?" This, I hope, will elicit some underground veins in his mine of memories.

He drinks long and hard from his beer can, puts it down with a clunk.

"Who knows." He shifts himself in the creaking chair again, and I'm afraid he's going to shut down, close off the access, but then he starts up again. "I thought about your mother and how she was, whether she'd got any news, and ... We'd been able to write a letter — I wasn't able to write, but a guy who'd been in there for a couple of years, he wrote the letter for me. To Mother, which she's got somewhere around here —" His hand waves and his eyes slide over the bookshelves across from us, as if he might that easily locate the letter written 50 years ago. The hand drops and the eyes wander out the window again. "And I wondered whether she'd got the letter, knowing whether I'm alive or whether they'd actually given it to the Red Cross and ..." He stops and shakes his head, then finally he shrugs, dismissing my question altogether. "You know," he says, as if I should — as if I could — understand. Then, after he thinks about it, he adds, "Who knows what I thought about?"

As I watch and wait, he tries once more. "Those things went all through your mind. Wondered about my own mother, whether she knew or Dad had told her or …" His voice, verging on trembling, breaks off.

I offer another question, to give him time to regroup or the chance to move on, go somewhere else in his memory.

"How long were you there?"

"I was only there for a month." As if it were no time at all.

And for some POWs a month would have been nothing, but because he is my father, and because I don't have any other way of saying, 'I admire you,' I qualify the dismissal: "Yeah, but I bet it felt like four years …"

"Yeah," he says, more mellow. "It felt quite long." The understatement of the day.

"The Americans liberated you?"

"Yeah. General Patton's army."

"So when they came, were they very —"

"A big negro outfit." He cuts me off to tell me this, a prominent detail in his memory.

"Were they noisy and boisterous and … ?"

"No."

"No?"

"No. They were quite upset about the fact that … our condition … That we were in the condition we were."

"In other words, they thought you should have been dining on steak every night?" The Hollywood version of war is still with me.

"No, I don't think that. They were kind of … They were upset about our condition. They tried to feed us immediately, and of course there was no way we could eat. The rations they gave us were too rich."

He drifts away again, and in the long interval while I wait, afraid to ask too much, the neighbours' dog yaps repeatedly and then annoyingly. Somewhere beyond the dog, kids squeal and splash in a backyard pool.

Eventually, hungry for more, I pose another question, tentatively, hoping to prod him into talking again. "So they shipped you back from Rheims to England, did they?"

"Mm-hmm."

"And from there to … ? You didn't come right away to Canada, did you?"

"Oh no. I got back in … at the end of September. I guess that was to Taunton. The U.S. Field Hospital in Taunton, in Somerset." A jumble of thoughts quiets him and he concentrates. Or maybe he is wandering.

"When did Mom find out you were coming home?"

His blue eyes look at me from somewhere far away, confused. It takes him several seconds to process my question and then he jumps in. "Oh, I phoned her as soon as I got to England. I got the adjutant to phone."

"So she didn't know until you got there, in fact, that you were —"

"I phoned the *manor* house!" He perks up, remembering again. His colour rises and he sits up taller. "Yes! And, uh, I guess your grandmother just couldn't …" He hesitates, then sniggers — disdainfully? — before continuing: "Couldn't *not* get hold of Elizabeth to say that I was alive. But she wouldn't — her own mother wouldn't! — come down with Elizabeth to see me. Your mother and Aunt Lettice, Uncle Phil's wife, came down."

"And Mom was very pregnant, wasn't she?"

"Yeah." He passes it off quickly. "So I got moved from there to an American hospital in Oxford, which was great because Mom was living in Oxford with the Hendersons."

"And that's where Charlie was born?"

"That's where Charlie was born, and it was shortly after that the Canadians caught up to me." He chuckles again.

"Why were they looking for you?"

"I was a Canadian in an American hospital and they wanted the Canadians in a *Canadian* hospital. So when they finally found me, they shipped me to a Canadian hospital north of London, in Watford Junction … And it was just like night and day. I mean, they treated you and fed you like kings in the American hospital. In the Canadian hospital you might just as well be cleaning floors. You got nothing." He shakes his head again. Out of shame for his country, I wonder? "Every day the PX at the American hospital would come in — *every day* —" he stops and looks at me to make sure I heard — "and say, 'Do you want some cigarettes, Brown?' 'I've got three cartons under my bed!' 'Oh, have another one!'" And he laughs at the fun of having outdone somebody, somehow, even if it was only the cocky Americans. "Then they'd say, 'What kind of candies you want?' 'Don't want any candies. Got two boxes of them under my bed.' 'Have another one!' And their food was just absolutely out of this world. Just *beautiful* food."

"So why was the Canadian hospital so bad? No money?"

"I don't know. They just didn't … I don't know! I mean, they didn't come around and offer you cigarettes. If you wanted some cigarettes, you had to go and buy them. And uh, chocolate bars were nonexistent. Oh, it was just …" He dismisses the memory with a whoosh of air, disgusted. "Oof! Just something else. Anyway, they wanted to operate on me, on my leg, in Watford, and I said, 'You're not going to touch me! I'm waiting 'til I get home!'"

"What made you think that the Canadian doctors over here were any better than those ones, though?"

"They were all …" He searches for a word. "Unskilled doctors, let's put it that way. This was a general hospital, eh? There was no way I was going to let 22- and 23-year-old surgeons touch me. No way!" When he says that, talking as if he's the expert and generalizing with characteristic self-assurance, I know that the horror of that 1944 night over France has passed for today. Now he remembers only the inconvenience, the pain, the tail end of that long, dark night.

Cold Feet

*T*he envelope from the POW camp was addressed by Eric, but when Elizabeth opened it, the handwriting inside was unfamiliar.

Eric hadn't wanted to write, had wanted rather just to drop out of Elizabeth's life. When he regained consciousness in the POW hospital, the seriousness of his physical state appalled him. His future, all his dreams, would have to change. For the time being, only his past remained alive.

~~~

Vancouver in the late 1920s was the end of the line, a dirt-road backwater.

"When I went to school," Eric looks at me from beneath a white brush of eyebrows, "you could walk diagonally from our back yard — I mean *diagonally* — down to Kitsilano Beach."

"Without going through people's backyards?" I am remembering the stories he's told me about the mischief he made as a young boy. Maybe he traipsed through the backyards of unfenced homes and got into trouble on his way to the beach.

"Without going through *any*thing. Just vacant lots. Very seldom did you have to walk along a block."

It's probably only a mile or so from Twelfth and Alder, where Fred and Eileen Brown raised their three boys, to Kits Beach, but I frown doubtfully, thinking my father must be exaggerating. He's a lot like his own father used to be, a lavish embellisher of stories from the past. I make a mental note to go to the library, find some photos to verify this description of 1920s Vancouver, unbelieving daughter that I am. It's difficult to imagine my father as a young boy, more difficult still to picture him wandering the familiar area of South Granville without its old office and tenement buildings, those three- to five-storey brick structures that used to dominate the area. It's hard to believe that Vancouver could have been any more sleepy than it was in the 1950s of my own childhood.

Something else occurs to me. "Did you live in the suburbs, then?"

"Yeah!" He snorts it out.

"There was no Richmond in those days?"

"Oh, hell no! Richmond was all farms."

"Where was the end of the city, then? The southernmost limit?"

"41st Avenue. From there on it was all dairy farms. Going north up Granville or Oak Street, the streetcar lines were on the extreme west side of the street. There weren't two tracks. There was just one track."

"The streetcar ran back and forth?" My ignorance is embarrassing even to me.

"Yeah."

"And it stopped at 41st?"

"No. It went down an old gravel road, a dirt road, all the way to Marpole. The Eburne Sawmills were down there. Marpole used to be called Eburne, eh?"

The Vancouver that Eric grew up in sounds like a pioneer town to me, child of the space-age '50s. He tells me about the coal-gas stove in their house on Twelfth Avenue, the icebox on the back porch, the delivery man with his huge tongs and leather bag, oversized ice cube on his back, struggling up the stairs of their back stoop. ("Cost Mom and Dad twenty cents for a block of ice.") The Chinaman who delivered vegetables in an open truck, and the horse-drawn cart of the Four-X Bakery. The milkman in his Model A Ford, the Jewish peddler clopping down the chestnut-lined street, walking beside his horse and wagon, calling out, "Junk! Junk!"

He remembers his Cecil Rhodes Elementary School teacher, a Miss E. L. Fant — "Guess what we called *her*!" — and Mr. Gibson, the rugby coach at King Edward Secondary School. He can also name the principal and vice-principal — "Daddy" Sanderson and Mr. Wilson — and Brigadier Ties, who taught chemistry. I listen, amazed at his memory, then saddened by my next thought: they must all be dead by now, these people he's remembering so fondly.

"I was a poor student." He laughs from the other side of my thoughts. "I always got at least 50 or 51%, but I'd only get an A or a B in subjects I liked."

He leans forward, searches for something in a file he has on the floor, hands me a sheet of paper. His high school report card. I look at the marks: English — 37%; Typewriting — A; Math — 77%; French — 50%; P.E. — C-.

"Why have they given you a C- in P.E.?" I ask, puzzled.

He shrugs. "Probably ignored the teacher and did my own thing."

There are few photos of Eric in his youth, but those that exist testify to his athletic abilities. In high school he played on the soccer, rugby, football and lacrosse teams, and he was an avid ice-skater. At UBC he played lacrosse at the provincial championships level. And when Doug, his oldest brother, introduced him to skiing, Eric joined the Grouse Mountain ski team and took up downhill racing.

They skied on the North Shore, hiking up to the top of Grouse Mountain with skis and packs on their backs.

"You *hiked* up?" My voice squeaks with incredulity.

I learn more then about the boy who became my father than I'd ever known before.

It was an all-day excursion to go skiing in the '30s. The Lions Gate and Second Narrows bridges weren't yet built, so the brothers took the car ferry across Burrard Inlet to the foot of Lonsdale Avenue and rode a streetcar to its final stop at the top of the hill. From there they had to hike across Mosquito Creek to the Grouse Mountain trailhead.

"The trail went up the mountain, all the way to the top, switchbacks most of the way. It was built during the Dirty Thirties, by people who ran out of work — they called them IRA camps. Even in those days we'd be packing up and we'd see these guys working on the trail."

They skied the base of the big hill across from the Grouse Mountain Chalet, on wooden skis with old bear-claw bindings. By the end of the day, tired from hiking up the slopes after each run, they had to hike back down the mountain and home.

When Eric lay in the POW hospital bed without his right leg, those days of skiing, of lacrosse and soccer fields, football and ice skating must have seemed like a dream. He lay on his back, blinded by the nausea and pain, hands and foot trembling, waiting for the sporadic doses of morphine the doctors gave him and worrying about his messy future.

It was another cellmate who urged him to write to Elizabeth. At first Eric refused, claiming it would be best to drop out of her life.

My mother has saved Eric's correspondence from the many months prior to his last bombing mission, letters full of the sentimentalities and inanities of a lover, a young husband full of hopes, plans and beliefs in their future together.

I cannot make the leap from his letter of June 11, 1944 — the last letter in the bundle Elizabeth put away after the war, the one that rambles on about where they'll be staying during his leave, June 20 to 25, and ends by telling her where his past week of "ops" has been spent: "*D-Day at Cherbourg, Tues. at Houlgate, Wed. at Conde-sur-Noireau, Thurs. at L'Orient, Fri. Paris, Sat. at Le Mans, Sunday in bed (oh boy!)*" — to the emotionlessness of the letter penned by his cellmate. Missing from Eric's two POW letters are the closing salutations from his previous correspondence as her "Very loving," "Very proud" or "Very lonesome" husband. Now he signs himself just "Ric."

The letter writer, a man whose name was forgotten in the rush of history following Patton's liberation of Rheims, must have been a person of great sensitivity. He sat beside Eric's bed and talked to him, urging him out of his depression and discovering his wife's name. Eventually he came to Eric with paper and pencil in hand. At the top of the paper he wrote, *Dear Elizabeth,* and then he told Eric he was going to write her. If Eric wanted him to say anything in particular, that other prisoner said, he'd better make it known.

───

GEPROFT, the stamp in the top left corner says: *EXAMINED.* And then the dainty handwriting, so much more legible than Eric's usual scrawl, begins:

There is something I will have to tell you. My right leg was amputated just below the knee.

Nothing more. No description of how he ended up c/o DULAG LUFT, GERMANY.

And then the subject changes abruptly and the tone becomes more like a child's summation of his week at summer camp:

I received a Red Cross parcel which was very good. There are tinned food (salmon, cheese, juice, etc.) ...

Beyond the shaky signature at the bottom is a postscript, this time in Eric's hesitant hand:

Take care of the little fella until I can get there. I'll bet he looks just like his momma.

Imagining his child was already born. Imagining a son.

But no signature after the postscript. Just a horizontal line and the word *Love,* the tail of the "e" falling off the page, exhausted.

Familiar Intimacies

The medical records in his air force file say this about Eric's leg: "This officer had his right foot blown off by a cannon shell while flying over Rheims, France, in a Halifax on 28 June 1944. As he baled [sic] out, he was struck by the tail of his aircraft, breaking the tibia and fibula in the lower third of his right leg. He was picked up by the Germans and taken to the German Prison Hospital at Rheims where on 29 June 1944 his leg was amputated (guillotine style) about seven inches below the knee. The wound was neglected and became infected. On 29 August 1944 the hospital was recaptured by the Americans. He passed through several hospitals and on 12 September 1944 the stump was revised and skin traction applied. Patient transferred to #23 Canadian General Hospital on 27 September 1944 and skin traction removed and stump bandaged.

"Patient is at present feeling unsettled, has lost weight and is anxious about stump of leg which has not healed completely. There is no pain and in general he has no definite organic complaint. The Surgeon recommends that the definitive amputation be delayed until arrival in Canada."

When Eric was shipped back to England, Elizabeth was due to go into labour. She'd tried earlier to enlist some help from home, but either Anthea or May, perhaps both, were indisposed to welcoming a baby at Coates, reasoning that "it would be too much work for the already depleted staff of servants." So Elizabeth stayed in Oxford and brought her newborn son to the tiny bungalow shared with Stella Henderson and Stella's month-old son. Shortly afterwards, Stella's husband Peter returned from the front with a shot-up knee. By the time Eric was released from hospital, the tiny Oxford cottage was filled to bursting with two new babies, two immobile veterans and two exhausted new mothers.

Peter, worried about Eric and Elizabeth's lack of family support, phoned Coates Manor hoping to arouse some sympathy for the young couple's difficulties at this time. He spoke to Uncle Phil there, telling him of Eric and Elizabeth's situation and asking if the Firths might be willing to help.

"Now that they're married, they've got to learn to stand on their own two feet," Uncle Phil told Peter.

And Peter, so we've been told over the years, spat out his own retort: "That's fine, but Eric's only got one foot to stand on!"

Eric left for Canada on November 14, 1944, aboard the No. 1 Canadian Hospital Ship. Elizabeth stayed in England, waiting for the Department of National Defence to arrange her separate passage as a war bride immigrating to Canada.

She spent her final few days in England at Coates. From a manor house burdened with silver, crystal and china, Elizabeth brought only six kitchen forks and knives with which to set up a new home in Canada. Anthea donated some towels and two pairs of the coarse linen bed sheets from Elizabeth's boarding-school days, but nothing else was offered.

"My fault for marrying a colonial. Out of my sort of world," Elizabeth explains with a wry face.

In January 1945, when baby Charlie was three months — old enough, according to government regulations, to manage the trip to Canada — Elizabeth arrived at Red Cross Headquarters in London.

In one arm she held her son, and in the other hand she clutched a suitcase with all her worldly possessions.

By February, they were on a train for "an unknown destination." That information was not given to the war brides or their families for security reasons. In Glasgow, on board the Cunard line's SS *Aquitania*, Elizabeth found herself in a cabin converted to 12 berths. Charlie, slung in a little hammock over her bunk, was the only child in the cabin.. The North Atlantic crossing was a grim experience: between being seasick and nursing the baby, Elizabeth had to deal with the antics of her cabin mates.

"They were all single, out for a good time and partying most of the night, waking the baby at 3:00 AM when they came to bed!"

The ship zigzagged up and down the ocean, windows blacked out as caution against submarine attacks. After ten days the *Aquitania* arrived in Halifax, where the women were removed to a train for Montreal.

In Vancouver, Eric had been referred to the orthopedic centre at Shaughnessy Hospital. On January 12, 1945, he was admitted for "further surgery to stump, further shrinkage and fitting of prosthesis." On February 17, he was released from Shaughnessy Hospital, still on crutches.

"What happened to your eye?" I ask him. "Didn't they do anything about that?"

"They couldn't do anything. It's the way it is and it's not getting any better or any worse."

"But even back then, couldn't they have done anything?"

"Nope. Didn't really start to go on me until —" Eric looks up at the ceiling and I follow suit, but there's nothing there "— the first year I was at Osgoode Hall," he finishes the sentence, lowering his eyes again.

"That was the year after you were back?"

"Yeah. That's when I started noticing. It didn't go just overnight. It got progressively worse to the point where, when I finally got back out here — I was still fine, able to see to a point — but about the second or third year of my practice I really had a problem. I was doing a lot of night studying and briefing, things like that. I finally went up to the hospital and said, 'Hey — there's something terribly wrong here.' What had happened, apparently, was a piece of shrapnel or flak — whatever the hell it was — had lodged itself back in here somewhere." He holds his stubby finger to his left temple, like the barrel of a handgun, and I nod quickly so he'll remove it.

"Do you have vision in that eye now?" Funny to be asking my parent a question most children would know the answer to.

"No," his voice slides from a high note to a lower one, doubtful, "I can ... see dark and light."

"But you can't see actual detail."

"No." I hear the same sliding intonation and I wonder if he is feeling defensive. I think of him driving the wet, grey streets of Vancouver, this old man. Has he memorized his routes or can he see well enough to drive? When we talk about him getting old, this is what my sister and I discuss, shake our heads over. Are we, knowing about his poor eyesight, responsible for curtailing his determination to continue driving? Do we have the right to play God?

Instead of a reprimand, though, I offer him something else to consider. "That puts a strain on your other eye, I guess."

"Oh, it's fine, the other eye's fine," he insists. "I'm nearly 20-20 in the other eye." He says it with such assurance that I feel a twinge of pity, remorse for what is inevitable: the loss of independence that he, and we, will have to face some year soon. But I give him a weak smile of complicity as he shakes his head in absolute denial. "No, the doctor — the eye specialist — said to me, 'So long as you can see light and dark, it *won't* put a strain on this eye because that eye is still concentrating on what it's looking at."

"Is there a possibility, then, that wherever the shrapnel or flak is, it might dislodge itself and the vision could come back?" I know I sound hopeful, but I tell myself it is for him, not for me.

"It's severed something." He says it without any emotion, but with a finality that sounds like a warning. "What it was, what it is, they don't know."

"Do you still have pieces of shrapnel surfacing in your skin sometimes?"

"Mm-hmm."

"How often does that happen?"

"Not so often now."

"It used to happen more often?"

"Oh yeah, quite often. Matter of fact, the last one came out right here." He rolls up the sleeve of his T-shirt to show me the fleshy part of his underarm. I try to be enthusiastic, but I'm embarrassed at this intimate sight of my father. There is a slight scarring, a dark shadow where the metal escaped from his body.

He rolls the sleeve down again. "I haven't had one come out for a long time. I think it's about two or three years ago since one came up."

I am aware, as I think he must be too, that we are dancing somewhat politely around a whole sewer of shrapnel, filling the cassette in the tape recorder with stuff I don't really need instead of digging into the real mine.

And then, suddenly, we are talking about death again.

"This is what happened up here." He turns his head and slides his index and third fingers along the bone behind his ear, and I am transported to that time, not long ago, when my siblings and I crowded around my mother, sure that this was the end. "This is why I had to have these two operations. There were five pieces of shrapnel accumulated around the parotid and then —" He pauses, looking for a word, nods when he finds the right one and continues. "Nature formed a cyst around them, and the cyst kept getting bigger and bigger and bigger, and the same thing over here." He moves his fingertips, places them behind and below the other ear, on the neck. "So they had to go into the parotid and cut them out."

He tells me this matter-of-factly, sounding as methodical as a doctor, as if there was never anything to be worried about. But what I remember is a long, fearful wait.

Winter, 1991. Over a dark succession of cold days we waited for the call from the hospital, the notice for Eric to present himself at Admitting. We sat in the family kitchen, my sister and I, drinking tea and trying to keep our spirits up. We spoke in low voices, whispered fears about what might happen during surgery so close to a major artery. Our eyes flicked back and forth from each other's face to the doorway, watching for Eric's sudden appearance from the room next door where he sat in front of some eternal football/hockey/baseball game with his glass of wine. We didn't want him to hear our talk about neurosurgery at his age and in his condition, the possibility of paralysis or hemorrhage from a tiny slip of the scalpel, where he might have to be moved to if things went wrong and who would stay with Elizabeth through the transitional stage.

We never considered that a man who'd parachuted through a flak-littered French night into the grey days of morphia might already know the pain of death. Never considered that Elizabeth was already more experienced at losing him than we would ever be.

Arrival

*D*espite all these exhumations of family, I'm still unsure of my home.

I'm still unsure how Elizabeth, the well-brought-up English girl, came to be so comfortable in the Canadian bush, so far from the chintz drawing rooms and civilized manners of English society.

I picture my father, droning through the night sky in a camouflaged bomber, and my mother, rumbling across an uninviting land toward a strange future, and the size of their risks amazes me. During the last few weeks of 1944, when Eric was already in Vancouver preparing for rehabilitation surgery, his mother wrote to Elizabeth to suggest that maybe she shouldn't come to Canada. *Eric does not seem ready to settle down*, Eileen Brown penned in her very precise, very careful hand. But Elizabeth, her passage already booked, was undeterred.

This is where Darwin's theory of evolution must have come from, I think: in the adaptation of the species there must be those who choose to give up everything in order to survive.

~~~~

February 1945. Coast-to-coast snow. "The scenery was monotonous," Elizabeth says of that inaugural train ride across Canada, "but I was spurred on by the prospect of seeing Eric again." So far from home, so much of nothing outside the train window, and she turns to the warmth of that homing instinct in her breast.

"We pulled into the CPR station in Vancouver and the whole Brown tribe was there to meet me. I had hoped for just Eric alone but realized it was a nice gesture of solidarity." She smiles, almost sadly I think, before continuing. "And then a reporter pounced on me. 'What do you think of Canada?' I'm afraid I said, 'I haven't seen anything but snow so far,' which was obviously not the right answer. I should have gushed a little bit." She stops when I wrinkle my brow in puzzlement, then explains, "People didn't think much of war brides generally. So many foreign girls had married servicemen for their big paycheques." She shrugs, remembering how careful she'd had to be of these strange Canadians and their feelings.

I smile at her, shake my head in chagrin. But there is something else she is not mentioning, something I found in the old metal box my father gave me a while back.

At first there seemed to be only layers of sentimentality in that box: an autographed program for the Government of B.C.'s June 3, 1938, "Champions of British Columbia Banquet and Ball"; a pale-blue Victory Bond envelope with the return address of my grandfather's first drugstore, *Capitola Pharmacy, cor. Davie and Bute Streets, Vancouver, B.C.;* the deed to a grave lot at the Vancouver Masonic Cemetery for which my grandfather paid $110.00 in 1925; a small brown glass bottle of Alophen (Aloin, Strychnine, Belladonna leaves and Ipecac) from Parke, Davis & Co., Walkerville, Ontario; a small red leather book of recipes for such wonders as the "City of Vancouver Ear Wig Mixture," a gonorrhea cure and "Dr. T. P. Hall's Magic Lotion."

But underneath those forgettable souvenirs, I found two brown paper envelopes containing some negatives and prints. Black-and-white shots of my father in rolled shirt sleeves and suspenders beside his motorbike — an old Indian? — licence number BLK 97; my father and his air crew on the wing of the Halifax bomber, their bodies less than a quarter the size of the huge propeller blade beside them, leather jackets open to show the warm fleece lining; my father at the controls of the Halifax, the wind whipping his hair so that he has a waterfall like Elvis Presley's. These never-seen-before pictures were buried treasure for me, revealing more clues about my unknown father.

And then I uncovered the last photo in that skimpy pile and felt my eyes grow big with surprise. In my palm lay a rare shot of my parents, Eric on crutches, Elizabeth in a shut-eyed swoon, the two of them in a passionate embrace, their shadows on the riveted siding of a train behind them. Overwhelmed, it took me a full minute to recognize the occasion. The reunion kiss.

Holding this evidence of unfamiliar intimacy between my parents, I felt exposed, as though I'd been caught spying. The weight of the moment, both past and present, made my hands tremble, and I laid the photo on the table in front of me, stared at it as though it was something illicit. Or fake.

Even now, I see in the photo how Eric leans into Elizabeth, a leather-gloved hand squeezing her very slim waist. How my mother's arms hang limp, wedding-ringed fingers clutching her slipping handbag as a rakishly feathered hat threatens to slip from her tilted crown of curls. Their eyes are closed, but his stance, the other gloved hand pulling at her rib cage, is hungry.

There was only the briefest of moments for Eric and Elizabeth to treasure this reunion. Eileen, who went out of her way to ensure that her name or photo was in the social pages whenever possible, had invited a reporter from the Vancouver *Sun* to participate in the welcome of her English daughter-in-law. Elizabeth's initial impression of Vancouver society, therefore, was via a brash young man breathing fast questions into the circle of new family clustered around her.

But even I devour the patent intimacy of the reunion photo without concern for the couple's privacy. When I realize how hungrily I am staring at my young parents, a hot shame floods over me.

Was it the aspiring young cub who shot that reunion kiss, I wonder? Was it he who caught the visual evidence of their missing past, a passion I would never have believed possible?

Or was it Eileen who caught the kiss on film and gave it to the newspaper? The possibility makes me shrink from any association with her, this woman who dies less than a decade after the photo is taken and who leaves nothing but three lost boys. Eileen is a grandmother I have not grown to care about, a relative I am connected to by blood and genes and idiosyncracies but about whom even my father, when I ask him what he remembers of her from his childhood, can only say, "She was a wonderful person. A wonderful person."

I learn from this that we leave only feelings after our passing.

It was a hard adjustment for Elizabeth in her new world. After the joyful reunion and meeting with her new family, real life and its litany of sorrows set in.

"It was so different here ... People ate early — very working class — and sat around and drank all night. Rye and ginger ale — ugh! We were the only ones with children ... I was the spoilsport who always wanted to leave early because of the baby ... Eric's father told people that I referred to a roast as a 'joint,' and Eileen told them my mother drove a Rolls Royce ... It was a new kind of snobbery for me, totally based on money ..."

She ends, finally, by sighing. "It must have been a very hard time for Eric, having a funny wife who was 'different' and didn't really belong ..."

She pauses, and I imagine the loneliness that must have been starting even then for her. But she sits up suddenly, remembering something else from that first year in Canada. "And one night there was this big thunderstorm. A huge blast of lightning crashed at the window, and Eric and I *leaped* out of bed to grab the baby and dive under the bed, thinking it was an air raid." She turns to me, a sheepish grin on her face, and I wince, unable to tell her how touching that picture is.

The memories start to come fast and hard now, and though I want to stop and ask questions, I let her go, hoping to catch up later.

She tells me about their first Vancouver home, a tiny bachelor walk-up, a real find in a wartime city with zero-vacancy. She smiles wistfully as she recalls, "The oven door was kept shut by a chair propped against it. And I had to learn how to clean things myself." She shakes her head. "I had to learn to squelch the nausea at having to scrub toilets, of all things."

Her pensive mood returns.

"Eric had a hard time learning to walk with his first wooden leg, and I had to learn not to try and help or show sympathy when he fell flat on his face. Not an easy time. I never wrote home about any of this. Mother wondered why I didn't write, but there was nothing cheerful to write about." She grows quiet and her eyes water. When she turns to me, they soften. "I used to hope none of my children would be foolish enough to marry someone from a different continent because it was so lonely. Marriage is hard enough without big cultural differences on top of normal adjustments, let alone a disablement to cope with."

I nod, struck dumb by the size of the mountain Elizabeth chose to climb.

Buried Memories

*T*oward the end of the interview tapes, I can hear that Elizabeth has lost most of her accent, relinquished yet another of her ties to Britain. And after half a century in the colonies, she no longer has that peculiarly English ability to deliver a passionate speech without revealing emotion in her facial expression. Now she is unable to speak without wrinkling her nose, curling her lip or raising an eyebrow to underscore the meaning of her words.

Elizabeth arrived in Canada to the disappointing realization that the Browns were, according to English standards, very lower middle class, "not much above shopkeepers." But since she'd committed herself, she was determined to fit into the new world she'd come to.

One of the skills she had to learn in her new country was a level of conversation more appropriate to working-class society.

"With the Browns, for instance, I couldn't say, 'Have you been to the Louvre recently?' or 'Have you read a book by so-and-so?' because they'd obviously never read anything much beyond Harlequin romances." Elizabeth laughs, somewhat bitterly, then frowns. "It's so hard to explain. It was just different." She waves her hands in the air and adds dismissively, "Different, different, different."

She shakes her head, frustrated perhaps, or embarrassed, and I can see that I've made her uncomfortable by talking about those details that reveal her foreignness, her elitist tendencies. But I don't know how else to get at the core of this enigma, the radically different way Elizabeth views things and the discomfort that difference has always caused me about my English heritage.

"Eric's mother was very kind to me always. But she was the most ghastly snob of anybody I've ever met. She told all of her friends that I came from this terribly rich background! I mean, I was brought up that you *never* talked about money, and you certainly didn't go around telling people you were rich."

"Snob" has a very different meaning for my mother than it has for me. I would have said *her* family were the snobs. Anthea especially, who was unable to have a conversation with anyone beneath her class, automatically looked down on certain people as being "rather common" and didn't believe that those outside her limited society had anything interesting to say. Elizabeth agrees that her mother was a snob, but qualifies it as "different." Her classification makes me wonder about other levels of snobbery, about whether there are, in fact, two sides to my family's snobbishness.

"Money snobbery is just not on, you know." Elizabeth looks at me from beneath a slight frown, challenging me to agree, and I nod briefly, not wanting to influence the direction of her conversation. It is a touchy subject, this — one we've skirted for many years. Her expectation seems to be that because I've benefited from an upper-class background, I should want to protect that status by maintaining distance from the lower classes. But though I've inherited some of the glitz and finery of my English ancestors, I feel a responsibility to obliterate the small-minded attitudes and oppressive behaviours that went hand in hand with their ostentatious lifestyle.

I put the problem aside for the moment as Elizabeth calls me back to the 1940s.

"I had to go to all these parties and things and everybody thought I was rolling in diamonds, and here I was, this rather frumpy young woman in a very ordinary dress. Eric and I hadn't got a penny to rub together and they all thought we should be fearfully rich. It was devastating to try and live down what Eileen had said."

It was even harder when one of Elizabeth's new sisters-in-law sneered, "Anybody can come to Canada and bring a photograph of a big house and say that's where they lived …"

Eileen, the woman whose son remembers her with a faraway gaze and a tendency to embellish her memory, was a person who kept her own mother shut in a third-floor bedroom, telling her to stay out of the way. A woman who played her daughters-in-law against each other, spurring rivalries between the three couples and their wives. And a woman who, when her third son, my father, was born, turned her face to the wall and didn't respond to the doctor's announcement of another healthy boy. Didn't speak, didn't hold out her arms to cradle the tiny life, didn't even cry. And that small, wrinkly infant so carelessly ignored, growing into a man so completely unaware of the deep scar left by his first meeting with Mother.

It is difficult to imagine a loveable side of Eileen, the grandmother who died in the early 1950s. Outside Eric's memories, Eileen stands like a sinister blackness in the family, most stories hinting that her personality fostered a lingering resentment in others. She hid behind the filing cabinet in husband Fred's office to catch him with his mistress and then coached the boys to make their father feel guilty about his behaviour. When Elizabeth and the baby first arrived in Canada and the young couple stayed with Fred and Eileen, Eileen showed no interest in her first grandchild, never held or fed him or offered to stay with him so the young couple could go out. And after Buster — the second son and Eileen's favourite — married, she encouraged him to come for lunch every day, pointedly reminding his new wife who was the first woman in Bus' life.

"Nobody ever talked about things in that home." Elizabeth wears a grim look as she shakes her head at this memory. "I doubt if there was ever much show of affection." The irony of this judgment does not escape me and I cannot resist probing.

"Well, that was the norm in your home too, wasn't it?"

And she turns to me then with a look that makes me sag. I see her pain — am confronted by the realization that my comment has caused it — and quickly shut off my own emotions in a self-protective reaction. I blink rapidly, trying to shield myself from the steeliness in her eyes, and when she speaks, I maintain a blurred vision, trying to distance myself from the thick slag of numbness in my belly.

For a moment she says nothing. Then: "It's just that both of us happen to come from families that were a very cold lot of people. Not loving and affectionate in any way."

I try to shift the focus by offering an excuse. "But the English have a reputation of being —" I shrug "— cold, don't they?"

Elizabeth turns away from me, looks out the window at the green boulevard in front of the living room window. When she looks back, her face is tired and the softness in her voice is wistful.

"I don't think you can classify a whole nation that way. I think the upper class are always rather a little distant because they …" She pauses and the silence underscores her helplessness. "Maybe because they have their children brought up by nannies."

I remember Elizabeth telling me how when she was young, she'd been led downstairs by her nanny each afternoon to visit with Anthea, Mary and Bernard, as if she were a guest and not part of the family. Later she would be whisked back to the nursery for her evening meal while the adults had tea.

And another story, about how the servants in other households, "nice old parlour maids and cooks," had been treated just like members of the family. She'd described those employees somewhat longingly, but then, as now, her voice had hardened, remembering a very different experience at Coates Manor.

"The cook locked the storeroom so that if I wanted an apple or a handful of raisins I'd have to go and beg for them." Elizabeth's face as she speaks, nose wrinkled in remembrance, portrays something so cold and so hard that I find myself remembering how it felt to be little and "in the way." I can hear the grumbling of the cook as she fussed about having to stop what she was doing, unlock the storeroom and find "the child" a snack.

I find myself considering whether the attitude that children are a bother was somehow unconsciously repeated in our house. The thought makes me instantly tired — tired of how all the childhoods seem so dismal, no matter which side of the family I look at.

Fathers, Sons, Family Ghosts

*S*ometimes my father's tone warns me not to believe what he says. He is just a touch too loud or too insistent about some particular detail, and at those times I begin to suspect his manipulation of the past. When it happens I wince with embarrassment, wanting to ask him to stop exaggerating. But what I do instead is much worse: I sit with a kind of glazed look, feigning admiration and letting him think I'm impressed.

It happens now.

~~~~

"My dad, regardless of his downfall," Eric says, referring to Fred's huge losses in the stock crash of 1929, "was very influential in the city. You'll see this in some of those files there." He waves toward a new pile of papers he's given me and I shudder, afraid of what I'll really find there.

I turn the pages of the notepad in my lap, find a fresh one and then look up at him, nodding agreeably.

"Dad knew *every*body. It was just too bad that the Depression came along, you know." He shakes his head. "Who the hell knows what Dad would have made of himself otherwise?" He sits up and his chest expands as he looks right at me. There is a hint of defiance in the look, daring me to challenge him.

I search for my pen, scribble notes to myself as I wait for something more. When nothing comes, I look up and catch him staring at me.

Waiting for an answer? I smile quickly, reach for my list of questions and, as I scan them, wonder how often my own lies have been as transparent as my father's.

I change the subject. "Why did you go to university right after high school when most of your friends joined the work force? Why didn't you go to work too?"

"I can't tell you why. I had no goal to obtain. I was just there because some of my friends were there, playing basketball, playing rugby. I was quite disinterested in the courses I was taking. Can't even tell you what they were. I suppose the war was a blessing in disguise, because when I got out, I was pretty well grown up. And then I knew *exactly* what I wanted to do."

Amazing to think that a war can help with the crucial decision of what to do in life.

He was 21 when they sent him home from England. Within the year, the Canadian government had offered its war veterans the choice of a free education or a house and land in appreciation for service to their country. Eric, who had returned from the war wanting to be a lawyer, applied and was accepted at Osgoode Hall, Canada's only law school at the time. In the middle of the summer of 1945, Eric and Elizabeth headed for Toronto.

Elizabeth's memories of life in the east are bleak. "We lived in various apartments in old houses. No one wanted kids there, and the summers were scorching in those rooms under the roof," she remembers.

We look at some black-and-white snapshots taken in those early years. As she speaks, I turn a page and see my oldest brother stuffed into a snowsuit on a wintry street.

Something shifts in her voice then. "Most places people speak to each other, especially with youngsters. But not in Toronto, 1945. No sir." Her voice drops to a whisper. "I just about died of loneliness. I would've given anything for someone to talk to …"

A thickening lump lodges in my throat as I stare at the young woman in a feathered hat, ankle-high boots and football-shouldered overcoat. I try again to read the distance between the smile in the picture and the words in the air. I look at the tired lines on the young face in the black-and-white photo and then, behind my right shoulder, I hear her say, "I took myself to church there at Christmas, but cried so hard I had to go home. Didn't go again for years!"

When I turn to look at her, I see my mother's skewed smile, and I have to force myself to swallow hard in order to stop my own tears. This pain I feel has no place in the resurrection of her memories. I bury it beneath other memories, those years of hardness that were to come much later.

They were always short of money in Toronto, despite Eric's government grant and disability pension. Toward the end of the month Elizabeth would buy a big soup bone and some vegetables in order to see them through the last week. The upper-class girl who had learned to live on a weekly paycheque of £3 during the war was both challenged and frightened by her slim new existence. The difficulty of their life began to eat away at them, because later that year Eric was admitted to hospital for ulcers.

"His mind was totally obsessed with getting the law degree," Elizabeth tells me, "and he said he couldn't study with me and two kids in that tiny apartment." She stops and a pained expression passes over her brow. "He has a habit of saying, 'I *sent* you back to my parents,' which I always rather resent because I didn't think …" She laughs nervously, then shrugs. "I don't think he sent me back. I went on my own accord." She pauses, then tries once more. "I think perhaps he was so …" When she hesitates again, I feel the slow tightening of my neck muscles. "… he was just so tense. About the whole thing."

I raise my eyebrows questioningly, unclear about "the whole thing" she refers to.

Elizabeth lowers her eyes briefly in a final attempt to explain. "I don't think he was very happy in Toronto. All the law students at Osgoode Hall were snooty young men who belonged to well-known families or law firms in the east." She sighs, a heavy release of air from the lungs. "I suppose they looked at him as some sort of upstart pipsqueak from the wild west, you know."

She left Eric in Toronto and went back to Vancouver to stay with Fred and Eileen, this time with two young sons. Christopher, born in December of 1946, was less than a year old when they left Toronto.

But when the University of B.C. opened its new Faculty of Law in 1948, Eric returned to Vancouver for his third and final year of law school. In 1949, after a year of articles, Eric opened his own practice at the corner of Pender and Howe in downtown Vancouver. He joined the Gyro Club, capitalizing on his father's social connections to build a clientele. He worked 18-hour days, and, with Elizabeth filling in as part-time secretary at the small firm, the boom years began.

When Eric first returned to B.C., he took out a loan with which to buy a small house in need of repairs.

"He worked very hard to fix up that house and sold it for a profit," Elizabeth tells me.

With the money he made, Eric bought another small house in Kerrisdale, where he and Elizabeth moved with my two brothers. On the top floor of that Elm Street house were two rented rooms whose income helped pay the mortgage. Around the same time, Anthea decided to give Eric and Elizabeth some money.

"It was £10,000, about $4.43 to the pound, when we got it out here. So for a while we invested it for a little income while Eric finished off at university, and then we bought a piece of land."

The land was a huge view lot in the undeveloped University Endowment Lands next to UBC. In the early 1950s, the tip of Point Grey was still predominantly forested and a 300- by 150-foot piece of the uncleared hillside sloping toward Spanish Banks cost them $7,200. Their friends were shocked at the amount they had paid for land without a house on it — but what a view.

Prior to receiving Anthea's gift, Eric and Elizabeth had often spent Sunday afternoons driving around the new roads and subdivision of the UEL, pacing the staked lots and fantasizing about their dream home. Early in 1953, they began to frame the three-storey brick and cedar-sided house that was to become our new family home.

~~~

In later years, Elizabeth said that Eric had built the big house on the Endowment Lands as proof to Anthea that he could provide as well as any of the Firths. Of course it was not the same, could never touch the lifestyle at Coates Manor, but for Vancouver in the 1950s, it was impressively big, though a strange mix of modern and idiosyncratic ideas. Most of the money Anthea donated went to the cost of building materials and so when construction was finished, the interior didn't quite live up to the surrounding locale, other grand homes of impeccable design and furnishings.

The heart of the house was Elizabeth's state-of-the-art kitchen with its deluxe General Electric appliances, even a dishwasher. The kitchen lay on the northeast side of the main floor to catch the morning sun. And because Elizabeth liked a bright kitchen, the walls were painted a butter yellow and the counters covered in a matching shade of arborite flecked with black.

There was a Dutch door in that first kitchen, a door that fascinated my sister and me. Whenever we were without entertainment, we hung on the lower half of the door, slumped over it neckless, like the two-dimensional green and red monkeys in a popular children's game of the time, grabbing with our toes at the bevelled edges and swinging back and forth until Elizabeth looked up from her ironing and reminded us that it was not a good thing to do — the hinges might break.

All of the windows in that big house opened and were situated so that a brisk cross-draft of the winds sweeping down Howe Sound and across Burrard Inlet could be caught and funnelled through the house. We grew up with the English notion that fresh air is a prerequisite to health.

At the bottom of the stairs, a long hallway tiled in black-and-white linoleum stretched from one end of the house to the other. When I stood at the doorway of the den and peered down the hall to the distant kitchen, I could blur my vision and see that orderly pattern of black, then white, then black again stretching reassuringly into the future. And on bored days of summer holidays, whenever the floor got polished with real floor wax (*Beautiflor* — *paste wax you pour*, sang the housewife on the TV set), we sprinted down the hall in our socks, stopping halfway to see how far we could slide — sometimes as far as four or five feet — laughing and spluttering as we crashed into the walls to stop.

Through large picture windows on the north side of the house we saw the freighters and sailboats coming and going in Burrard Inlet. And while Elizabeth cooked dinner in her new kitchen, we sat at the kitchen table and watched as storms gathered in the distance, churning up Howe Sound and dusting the scree-covered peaks of Hollyburn Ridge with the first snows of the season.

With my back to Burrard Inlet and Hollyburn Ridge, where as a boy my father had hiked all the way to the top so he could ski down its slopes (but when I looked at that blue, blue ridge of mountain, I thought he must be teasing me again; why didn't he go up the chair lift or the rope tow?), I could watch the laundry in the glass-doored washer and dryer beside the Dutch door. On empty, rainy days, with no one but my sister for a playmate, I'd sit at the table, filling in the pages of my *Barbie and Ken* colouring book and listening to the repetitive slosh-slosh of water in the washer, feeling comforted by the rhythmic noise. One day we heaved the still-wet mass of clothes from the dryer to insert a shoe box lined with soft tissues, a baby bird nestled inside the box. I don't remember where the lost chick came from, whether it had fallen from its nest or one of our huntress cats had stolen it from its parents, but I remember calling to my mother to come see it.

And I remember how her hands folded gently around the ugly baby, and how her voice turned quiet and soothing so as not to frighten the chick any more than it already was. We watched and listened as she explained, tucking the box into the well of the dryer, that the dark and the warmth in there would calm the baby, make it feel like it was still at home in a warm, feathered nest.

It was one of those episodes that convinced me my mother was very wise, that she knew what she was doing. Someone who could identify a grey lump of feathers as a baby robin or a baby chickadee, I thought, must be very knowledgeable about life.

In a Family Way

*I*n those early post-war years, the University Endowment Lands were a microcosm of the real world beyond their entry gates. Two long, shaded boulevards divided the area into three separate factions, delineating by environment the rich from the poor. Chancellor Boulevard separated the north-western sector of larger, sedate homes from a middle section of less ostentatious bungalows. Those more modest homes were in turn isolated from the blocks of older, tenement buildings — housing for university students and junior faculty — by the narrow lanes of University Boulevard. And all three areas were so distinctly removed from the city as to maintain the feel of a separate township.

There were advantages to living outside the official boundaries of Vancouver. In the late 1940s, at the beginning of the baby boom, the only way to educate the exploding school population was to operate city schools on a swing shift. In Kerrisdale, Elizabeth had been kept busy delivering one son to morning (9:00 to noon) classes and the other to afternoon (1:00 to 4:00) classes. But the two schools of University Hill, as the new subdivision on the promontory was called, weren't yet overcrowded, and so, for the first time, both of my brothers were sent to a full day of uninterrupted classes.

When it was my turn, I walked the three or four blocks to school beside broad lawns and manicured gardens without ever absorbing their advertising or understanding their significance. Carefully spaced shade trees of dogwood and maple branched and matured alongside my steps, but, like the well-worn clothes on some schoolmates, I never saw the discrepancies between my family and others. I knew that Vivien, a classmate, lived in the "Army huts," recruit-training buildings converted to student family housing after the war, and that Jimmy had no father at home — a fact of curiosity and some undiscussed kind of shame — but in the morning routine of elementary-school exercises I bent my head of tight braids alongside Vivien's unruly curls and Jimmy's Brylcreemed hair without an awareness of the huge gap of fortune between us. Each of us stood beside our respective seats in the joined row of one-size-fits-all wooden desks meant to accommodate various six-year-old bodies — as if we were all equal in the eyes of the school board — and recited the Lord's Prayer in choral unison. Sometimes I can still remember all the words to that recitation and I drone it off, try to recapture that feeling of being small, powerless, innocent.

When I was 11, I rode a bus downtown to go shopping at the Hudson's Bay Company with my friends, no fear of gangs or junkies on Granville Mall then. In the early 1960s, Vancouver was still a small town with none of the cosmopolitan aspirations that easterners like to scoff at today.

And University Hill, removed from Vancouver by a seemingly endless ride in the family's two-tone station wagon, so far away from the shadows of the only two skyscrapers, the Marine Building and the Hotel Vancouver, was another world altogether. After a day's adventure outside the small enclave, when the baby blue-on-white Buick slid up the long driveway at 1269 Acadia Road, we knew we were safe home. In a foreign land, perhaps, but home.

The university's presence didn't attract my attention until, during my teenage years, the possibility of meeting an older boy became a subject of conversations with girlfriends. As children, though, the roar of student traffic on both boulevards held serious threats when we walked to and from school, and if I went home with a friend in the afternoons, I had to call my mother to let her know I was alive and not one of the yearly statistics hit by drivers speeding to and from classes and part-time jobs. In the hallway of every friend's house, somewhere between the kitchen and the front door, I'd lift the universal black receiver of the 1950s to my ear and wait for the operator to say, "Number, please."

ALma 2-7880, I'd respond. The number that connected me to a strange English accent, so foreign yet so familiar, on the end of an identical black receiver in a yellow kitchen somewhere else on The Hill. The phone number for that blue-green house above the sea where my parents hoped to carve the good life.

And beyond Alma Street, the boundary between the telephone exchange for the University Endowment Lands and the rest of Vancouver beyond those stone gates whose presence announces the start of university lands at the western edge of the city, was our misplaced reality. Misplaced in more ways than my parents could ever have imagined.

When Eric and Elizabeth started the excavations for the house overlooking Howe Sound, my mother sent Kodachrome photos of the building site back to England. In pencil on the back she scrawled notes about the views and the neighbours. When the letter containing those photos arrived, Anthea would have taken it into her drawing room, seated herself at the wide double-pedestal desk and, reaching for her silver letter opener, fumbled at the seam of the envelope.

She must have pored over the snapshots, trying to imagine the place where her daughter had gone to live, trying to picture the faraway house being built in a strange land. Perhaps it was the proximity of the ocean in those photos, lingering behind the mounds of dirt and the skeleton of two-by-fours, or maybe Anthea had finally reached a point in life when the urge to connect was stronger than her dislike of the unfamiliar, but sometime during the construction of the house the aging woman who preferred the safety of home telephoned her daughter and announced a wish to visit Vancouver.

It was 1956 when Anthea ventured overseas on that first tentative trip to Canada. And she kept a journal in which she recorded her thoughts and reactions to the study in contrasts across the huge nation:

in May there were still a few icebergs in the St. Lawrence River, but two months later, going home, Montreal's heat was "intense." On the train ride west, there were "days of endless lakes before the terribly bare and monotonous Prairies." Anthea must have fidgeted then, losing interest in the vast country outside and wondering how her daughter found beauty in such a forlorn place — until that first breath-holding sight of the Rockies. And when the train stopped at the Great Divide to let the passengers see how the rivers flowed east on one side and west on the other, she wrote in her diary about the marvellous accomplishment of building a railway here "before all modern facilities were invented."

During Anthea's first trip to Canada, Eric was polite though not overly friendly to her. But while she was there, something seemed to ease the tension she felt toward her son-in-law.

Eric tries to explain it to me. "She hadn't wanted Elizabeth to marry beneath her social status, eh?" He turns, looking at me from beneath raised eyebrows to make sure I understand. "She actually tried to prevent the marriage." He shakes his head, pulls aggressively at his lit cigarette, and I watch the red ash flare, wondering about the nonverbal significance of this act.

"Did she ever say anything to you about it? About not being the 'right sort' to marry Mom?"

"No. But why else would she have had Uncle Mark check up on Dad here in Vancouver and find out that he went bankrupt?" He looks almost sad as he speaks about it, and I regret, again, the pain my parents have felt as a result of their families.

He shakes his head, clucks his tongue, resigned now to the scars from that time. Because Anthea, before she died, acknowledged Eric in her own gruff way; and however she accomplished that feat, it was apparently sufficient for Eric to relinquish his dislike of her. He has forgiven his mother-in-law and now remembers her only with regret.

Sometimes, now, Elizabeth is nostalgic for her lost past, lamenting her life at the edge of the colonies in spite of the new skills learned in Canada. She looks down on things like ready-made dry goods purchased at local department stores, "cheap and nasty" substitutes for the heavy silk brocade drapes and bedspreads so carefully sewn by Frithy, the old housekeeper at Coates Manor. And when she's upset, even small annoyances like "terribly poor service" at the post office or grocery store can set off a verbal harangue. Just like her mother, Elizabeth reverts to a very upper-class attitude, blaming bad quality on a lack of pride by contemporary workers.

And every so often she seems to need to reclaim part of that past. When I was young, she'd sometimes go on spur-of-the-moment shopping sprees, spending money indiscriminately because she "simply *must* replace" something or other, and then she was like a small child again, pleased with her new purchase and justifying its outrageous cost by explaining that the original was "simply *too* scruffy for words!"

These buying sprees were primarily a throwback to the days of going up to London with Granny May, shopping at Liberty's when money meant nothing and expense was damned. And when we were still children, a downtown shopping excursion was an event that Elizabeth would dress for as though it were an important social occasion: good coat, heels and a hat.

When Elizabeth came home from those impromptu shopping trips, dusk was already falling and it meant that dinner would be late, but her arms full of bags and newness and her face lined with tired contentedness said she was happy. The old way of life resurrected for just the space of an afternoon could do that, could give her a renewed sense of hopefulness about her changed lifestyle.

But then of course she'd feel guilty for her capriciousness. Maybe she would hear Anthea worrying about money again, or maybe her own conscience reprimanded her about the unnecessary waste of something worn but not completely useless. Then she would take the old bedspreads and tablecloths, the ones she'd bought replacements for, and cut them up for something else. Long curtains became short drapes or bedspreads for our beds; old dresses were made into blouses and skirts, old trousers into shorts.

The armchair I took with me when I moved into my first apartment was covered in material from the living room drapes of that big house overlooking Burrard Inlet, white woven stars splashed on heavy red wool. At night, in my teacherage beside the Squamish highway, I'd curl into that chair, cars and trains rushing away from me on their way to or from Vancouver or Whistler, and I'd dream of those childhood days in that big house, fitting pieces of memory together while touching the stars.

Relatively Speaking

*E*nglish relatives would venture across the Atlantic in sporadic bursts, staying with us in that big house on the Endowment Lands. In the weeks before their arrival, Eric and Elizabeth held disjointed discussions about what to show them.

"I phoned Harrison Hot Springs today," she'd mention at dinner. "Made reservations for the fourth. What do you think about trying to do the Hope-Princeton that same weekend?"

"Can't. Have a trial on the seventh. Why don't you just take them on a drive up the valley?"

"Pass the salt, please. Oh, I don't know."

The English family wanted the great Canadian wilderness, the postcard shot of the RCMP with the Rocky Mountains in the distance, so Eric planned trips to Banff, Lake Louise or the Columbia Icefield, and then he'd slip in a little extra, a fishing or hunting jaunt at some remote lodge he'd heard about. She would protest — "Oh really, Eric, they're not interested in roughing it!" — and he, hunched over the map, would shrug, continue his planning as Elizabeth turned away with a sigh of exasperation. His finger on a remote backwater of the Kootenays or the Chilcotins traced a route through the shadows of Nimpo Lake or the switchbacks of the unpaved Duffy Lake Road, somewhere no possibility of life, other than the wild variety, existed.

"If they want the real Canada," he'd say, "they have to get off the beaten track."

In 1961 Anthea came again to B.C., arriving in early September and staying through the end of October. Two weeks of that autumn were spent driving north with my father on his annual "hunting" (her quotation marks) trip for duck, prairie hen and grouse. They went up the Alaska Highway and into the Peace River country, "getting colder and colder." But the fact that Anthea agreed to go with Eric at all speaks to the fact that their relationship was growing — probably grudgingly, but improving in some measurable way.

Anthea's dislike of her son-in-law was not based purely on his colonial — and thus lower-class — background. He'd made some mistakes around his future mother-in-law which she'd been unable to forgive.

Once, during an early visit to Coates with my brothers, Eric had broken Anthea's shooting gun, a custom-made model from an exclusive London gunsmith. She'd loaned it to him the day the big field in front of The Thatched House was being harvested, when the reapers worked from the outside toward the centre in a kind of ritual dance. As the harvesters moved together, the wild animals who lived in the field — pheasants, badgers, hares and foxes — were driven toward the centre until, at the very last moment, they were forced to explode into broad daylight, fleeing from the workers' scythes. When told about this free-for-all, Eric asked to borrow Anthea's gun, a possession she undoubtedly loaned him begrudgingly. Eric shot at a hare, wounding it but unable to finish it off because of all the men in such close proximity. He raised the gun as he would an army rifle, intending to crush the skull of the still-kicking animal and put it out of its misery. But Anthea's gun was handmade by an artisan and not designed for crushing the bones of even the most delicate animal. When Eric threw his weight against the writhing fur, the butt shattered, breaking into wooden tears over the rabbit's head.

The incident did not endear Elizabeth's young man to his mother-in-law, especially since, even if he'd offered, he could not have afforded to replace the gun. But in 1961, with 2,200 miles of Canadian wilderness behind her, most of it spent with my father crashing over rutted logging roads through dense forests and unmapped backwoods opening onto some pristine lake miles from cold northern towns with strange names like Dawson Creek and Hudson Hope, Anthea fell in love with my father's country.

In her notes she underlines the word "marvellous" with a triple score, emphasizing, the way she would with her voice, the impression of "oil gushes burning in the night … sunsets and flights of ducks coming into cornfields against orange glows … golden leaves and scarlet berries quite lovely against the snow …"

Her last diary entry of the trip says it all: "The Peace River *too* incredible," as if she, like me, found the solitude of that country overwhelmingly alluring.

A few years after Anthea ventured west, Molly came for a visit. Once again Eric and Elizabeth drove into the heartland via the canyon and Molly rode the cable car across the Fraser River at Hell's Gate, her saucer-sized eyes peering out the glass of the gondola as it swung over the engorged spring river. Afterwards, my parents took her for hamburgers at the Cache Creek Dairy Queen, where the experience of eating without cutlery became one of the highlights of her west coast adventure.

Before they left Vancouver for that tour, Eric gave Molly a crash course on B.C. history. They sat in the May dusk of the living room, three shadows creeping across the blue shag carpet, and the women listened, sipping intermittently at Johnny Walker Red or Harvey's Extra Dry Shooting Sherry while Eric talked of forgotten places. Places like Yale, the final stop for paddlewheelers chugging up the Fraser River from New Westminster, bringing supplies and miners to the start of the 1858 gold trek. Or the coastal settlement of Roberts Creek, marked by the red pilings of a government pier where, in the days before community centres, the local population congregated to meet the twice-weekly steamship, its link to the outside world.

And when I went into the kitchen to hunt for a snack, I hesitated in the yellow light of the open fridge door, alerted by the drifting sound of that voice from the next room. My father the lawyer, who worked such long hours that the only time we saw him during early childhood was at the breakfast table, has always spoken in the ruthless, driving speech of the professional in court, grainy and brusque. But here, now, he was someone I didn't know, speaking in an unfamiliarly soft voice as he described a forgotten era of West Coast history. I listened from the dark of the kitchen to the almost-dreamy way his words fell like caresses on a lover, and for a second I was that lover, feeling the softness fold over and around me. It might have been then that I began to realize this is his land, his story.

But I was 15, too busy with the present and too impatient with grown-ups to care about the history he gave Molly on that visit. And while Eric and Elizabeth drove her over the legendary route of the gold rush, following the smaller highways into Barkerville and then home through the Kootenays, I was grateful for the break in my great-aunt's visit. In the thick of adolescence, I could find nothing to admire in her staunch Britishness, couldn't have realized that her constant zeal would one day touch my life. I knew only that Molly's rapid-fire questions about my daily life drove me to fabricate excuses in order to avoid conversations with her, leaving Elizabeth, Molly's surrogate daughter, to suffer with her intense presence. It was one thing, I felt, to put up with the ultra-conservative company of my English grandmother, but surely a great-aunt had no real claim to my attention.

We christened her "The Beak," as much to make fun of her owl-like features — two wide-set circular eyes and a small, pouted mouth — as her prominent Roman nose. The overly large appendage was, according to Elizabeth, an indication of breeding to Molly's peers, but in my circle of North American teenagers it seemed as comedic as a Groucho Marx nose-and-glasses set.

She presided over a room like a strong smell, a loud, ungainly and very unfeminine woman with a habit of speaking her mind at inopportune moments.

Bizzy and I were alerted to our great-aunt's faux pas by Anthea's frequently audible reactions to her sister. Whenever Molly blurted something inappropriate, Anthea would hiss with embarrassment or roll her eyes. One year Anthea took her sister for a birthday lunch at

London's famous Ritz Hotel. While ordering, Molly asked the waiter about the Dover sole. "Have you eaten any?" she asked. "Is it any *good*?" My grandmother told this story for years, as if to justify her impatience with her elder sister.

And Molly liked to inject her conversations with French phrases, that once-common practice of upper-class English households. But she was often forgetful of her French vocabulary, likely to substitute an English word in a foreign phrase, a habit that made her attempts at exclusivity more humorous than impressive. "*Prenez garde,*" she said one night at the dinner table during an adult conversation. "*Les murs ont* ears," sliding her eyes sideways to indicate my sister and me, then raising her eyebrows meaningfully at Elizabeth.

When Molly came to Canada determined to see a moose, she wanted to "do as the colonials." For her trip into the wilderness, she insisted on being taken to purchase a khaki hunting jacket and black gumboots, into which she tucked a pair of large-pocketed fatigue pants. She modelled her new outfit by taking a test walk (a "*test woke*") in the nearby woods of the Endowment Lands while I peered from behind the curtains, praying that none of my friends would drive by and notice the eccentric-looking figure outside the house. Those who had met her were already mimicking her speech, particularly the way she managed to make even the words "British Columbia" sound foreign.

Eric and Elizabeth told stories about Molly for months after each of her trips, my father laughing and shaking his head, my mother rolling her eyes in relief that the visit was "done" for another while.

Nearly four decades later, though, it's clear that Aunt Molly was the bridge between the chasm of my parents' backgrounds. The only relative on either side of the Atlantic unfettered by social expectations or family assumptions, Molly took great pleasure in flouting any social rules that discouraged personal aspirations. An Edwardian version of the in-your-face personality, she assumed she was welcome anywhere and made herself at home in most situations.

And in the oil-and-water mixture so naïvely combined by Eric and Elizabeth, Molly became the suspension agent.

Put to Rest

*M*olly visited Canada in 1966 or '67 and stayed with us in the much smaller house we had moved to after my brothers left home. She slept in my tiny bedroom, gold shag rug on the floor and dainty yellow roses on the wallpaper, while I removed myself to the basement, glad to get away from the adults, the weird English aunt, the dorky sister upstairs. I could play my stereo, Jimi Hendrix and Janis Joplin, keep my world separate from the straight one above and only have to socialize at mealtimes.

And Molly, needing something to do and horrified by the jumble in our compact (as compared to the English) linen cupboard, took it upon herself to reorganize and reclassify its contents, retraining us in the process. Each bed sheet, each tablecloth, each piece of nowhere-else-to-store-it length of material left over from various school sewing projects was swept off the crammed shelves and dumped in a heap on the floor. Happily distracted for a portion of the day, Molly folded towels, facecloths and pillow slips, matching corners and edges just so, replacing them on the wooden shelves now marked by a label written in her lanky, cursive hand. For several years, each time I opened those double wooden doors I'd see Molly's formal and stilted handwriting, so similar to that odd, foreign style of my mother's.

"Molly had lots of little books and lists of everything. She knew *exactly* how many tea towels she had and which year they were bought, where, when and how much she'd paid for them!" Elizabeth groans. "When she died I had books full of stuff like that and I *couldn't* keep them ..." She shrugs apologetically, knowing my covetous nature for all family records, the details that tell about character and idiosyncracies.

"And her linen cupboards had little lists stuck on each shelf and you didn't put the pillow cases here if they were supposed to be there, you know."

After the linen cupboard, my great-aunt discovered our untidy vegetable patch, screened from the swimming pool by a dense row of juniper and cedar. Molly, who spent "absolutely unlimited sums" on her own garden at The House on the Green, rearranged our small back plot by planting rows of vegetables and herbs, each marked by a short, flagged stick.

"Do you remember?" Elizabeth asks.

I don't, but I remember the garden at the back of Molly's home in Broadway, Worcestershire, and being sent to explore it while the adults had a drink before lunch. Bizzy and I passing through the two large-paned French doors at the end of the drawing room into a maze of gravel pathways and chocolaty earth, stepping tentatively on the crunching stones and moving past long stretches of waving stalks, both of us growing quieter as the house receded behind so much greenery. Each bush, each flower, each clipped shrub so proudly announced by black letters on short wooden stakes, words of indecipherable pronunciation and incontestable superiority. My sister and I, unnerved by the awful fastidiousness everywhere, afraid to run noisily through such careful order.

"Every rosebush had a proper label so you knew its genus and species, do you remember that?"

I remember looking at the unpronounceable words and wondering if my grandmother was right: What *were* the Canadian schools teaching us?

That was the day Molly served us a lunch of cold jellied meat, reinforcing the foreignness of this place, these relatives. And of course the dessert, when it arrived, underlining my growing discomfort.

"Now for a special treat!" Molly carried the serving bowl from the kitchen and set it before us with a glow of anticipation. My sister eyed the bowl in doubtful suspicion, and I had the sudden pregnant realization that as the eldest, the example-setter, I would have to *eat* some of the bowl's contents.

Molly, quite deaf with pride, ignored my request for a small helping.

"Here you go," heaping it into a large dessert bowl, "and more when you're ready for it!" Entirely unaware of the culinary tastes of North American children.

"What is it, Aunt Molly?" My voice full of doubt.

"Try some, dear." The voice of encouragement came from across the table, but I avoided my mother's eyes, my grandmother's hissed sigh.

"Gooseberry Fool — the gooseberries are from my own garden, right outside!" Molly served with gusto, spoonfuls of soft mush slopping against the china bowls. "You and Bizzy can go pick some more after lunch, if you like. Take some home with you." My sister's scared eyes, bulging like her weak stomach, looking at my mother with horror.

And I, feeling trapped by all those eyes, picked up my spoon and fork and poked daintily at the custardy slop before me, already having decided it was something I'd hate.

"Did you eat some of it?" my mother asks me now, biting her lower lip hopefully.

"I don't remember."

***

It's Molly's eyes I remember when I think of her now, their keen glint and sharp focus. I'm sure she never held it against me, but my biggest regret is not having taken the time to visit her when she was dying, for not having acknowledged her role in my parents' marriage.

My great-aunt Molly spent her last days in a nursing home. Whenever Elizabeth went to see her, she phoned first to ask if there was anything she could bring.

"I'd love a bottle of something, Lizzy," Molly would whisper over the wires and Elizabeth would stop at the Cirencester wine merchant en route to the home. The hospital didn't allow liquor on the premises, but Elizabeth felt sorry for an old lady who liked to break the rules.

"Aunt Molly loved a little nip at bedtime, you know," Elizabeth tells me with a confidential nod of her head.

And my sister, in England at the time of Molly's death, relates an eerie story of the night before the funeral. Awakened by noises downstairs, Bizzy tiptoed to the top of the stairs and listened. From the dense dark below, sounds of clinking glass wafted up the stairwell, "like someone opening the cabinet to pour a drink." The noise continued, but wary of the blackness at the bottom of the stairwell, Bizzy went back to bed. After several more minutes of the delicate noises, the mysterious sounds stopped. It was a long while before Bizzy fell back asleep.

In the morning she asked her house guest — a woman with strong psychic sensitivities — whether she'd heard anything the previous night. The response was a definitive, "No, nothing." Bizzy described, then, the noise of the rattling glasses, and her friend looked at her, judging, perhaps, whether it was safe to admit something.

"I didn't want to say anything yesterday evening, in case it scared you," the friend said, "but I saw somebody outside the dining room windows, looking in at us while we talked. A little old lady, big nose, round eyes …"

Molly, the great tippler, back for one last snort, we decided.

Personal Encounters

*D*uring the winter of 1970, I lived and worked in the noisy tumult of London, a sometimes frantic existence for which the antidote became an increased number of weekend visits to Coates. It is a part of my past that I try, with varying degrees of failure, to describe to my own daughter and which she can only imagine with the young person's foggy vision of the future.

But it's easy for me to travel back to that time — to be, once again, a 17-year-old living in a sixth-floor, walk-up flat …

Anthea's voice, when she calls, is soft and low, almost sultry, over the phone. Hailed by a roommate to the communal phone in my shared flat, I am carried by her voice up and over the blackened chimney pots crowding the windows of our top floor.

"Annie," she says, and I see her sitting at the lone black telephone of The Thatched House, installed in 1929 when she first moved there with my mother and never updated, never changed. She will have a view of the west garden in front of her, rows of yew trees, and behind them an extensively netted vegetable plot. Peas, beans, carrots, courgettes — the strange name the English give to zucchini — strawberries, raspberries, currants and gooseberries, all presided over by Wood, the gardener.

("You don't address outside workers, gardeners and such by their first name or by 'Mr.'," Elizabeth has told me. "You use their surname and it's not insulting or rude. That's just the way it is.")

"Hi, Granny," I chirrup back over the line.

"How are you, dear?" her voice as sexy as the slow cascade of chocolate syrup dribbled over ice cream. But the sound doesn't go with her face, tired and prematurely aged.

"Are you coming down this weekend?" she asks. "Should I do an extra shop tomorrow?" Perennially worried about supplies — "What can we *feed* them?" — Anthea never encourages visitors to stay for more than a cup of tea, a glass of sherry. Since there are no fast-food outlets in the Cotswold Downs, and no possibility that she would consider eating such stuff if there were, I am honoured to be welcomed in such a strange way.

Anthea, the shy recluse, loved her solitude. In the company of her closest acquaintances — Andrew, Coates' rector with whom she felt a shared responsibility for the spirituality of the parish, and Dorothea and Caroline, another friend who moved to Coates in Anthea's declining years — she could relax, be at ease with an unplanned visit. But with others, my grandmother exhausted herself, worrying about needlessly intricate details instead of enjoying the company and allowing a visit to unfold on its own. Part of her distress was due to a lack of experience entertaining people and a wish that someone else — preferably the help — could perform the less intellectual tasks, the shopping, cooking and preparing for a gathering or an event. But the other part of her distress stemmed from her desire for utter peace, a desire not to clutter her days with mindless bustling and constant chatter.

In the streets of Cirencester, the nearby market town where Coates' residents buy supplies, dank medieval shops with tiny windows of bubbled glass lean onto the sidewalk, sometimes forcing pedestrians into the narrow streets. Now whenever I return to England, I discover bright new premises beside the old establishments left catering to my grandmother's generation. Shiny yuppie interiors stand next to the dimly lit shops of butchers and green grocers, and outside their side-by-side entrances I am assaulted by sensory extremes. Through one door, behind dazzling displays of halogen-spotlit crystal, the enticing beat of syncopated jazz can be heard, and through the neighbouring door, an odour of gaminess precedes the shadowy sight of soft-eared hares and green-necked pheasants hanging from steel hooks. But these two extremes are normal somehow, and even the touristy part of Cirencester — the 14th-century cathederal and the cobbled roads and Roman ruins — are as familiar, as unnoticeable to me now, as the stunning mountain-and-ocean backdrop of B.C.

In the summer months, Cirencester's marketplace throngs with foreigners, and when a particularly drawled voice or large camera jostles me on the sidewalks, my grandmother's spirit reincarnates. Too many visitors annoy me.

Large busloads of tourists arrive daily to view the early Roman relics maintained by the Cotswold County and National Trust. Cirencester — Corinium during Roman rule — was the second largest city of Roman Britain, and the countryside around the ancient town is littered with the remains of villas, amphitheatres, roads and gateways. Governor Gaius, sent to Britain in the middle of the first century, intended Corinium as a military backup to London, and the extent of the ruins is evidence of his success.

The tourists burble muted oohs and aahs from behind cordoned-off mosaic floors and walls while monotone guides deliver memorized lectures, the details of which will be later forgotten or confused with details from other sites and towns on the visitors' tour. And because I feel that part of me is of this land, I become possessive of my territory, ridiculing the buyers of fake Roman coins and the rubberneckers beneath the imposing cathedral tower, resurrecting my grandmother's disdain for tourists and becoming another snob.

I am not like my mother, wanting to share the Cotswolds with all manner of foreigners, especially the Canadian friends and relatives who arrive at her enthusiastic invitation. While resident in England,

Elizabeth happily drives her visitors about, stuffing them full of facts and history, all they can hold in one day, five days, ten. But I horde my pleasure in the quiet of the green countryside, wish the tourists and outsiders would go away, stay away.

That is how I feel today, though. At 17, living in the great city of London, I was not so jaded.

⁓

On Fridays, the soot-covered walls of Paddington are crammed with crowds of solitary lives rushing to leave London. After the panicked press of late boarders, the old BritRail engine choofs out of the station past the blackened brick slums and barbed-wire-fenced tracks, leaving London and its poor for the weekend. At Reading, where I change to a small commuter train that lurches and gags along a slow track, the Huntly Palmer Biscuits sign and two towers of a nuclear power station are the final urban scars before the train carries its evening load, now gilded by the setting sun, toward the oncoming dusk. Past empty fields and into a tunnel, surprising huddled rookeries with the scream of steel on steel, we blast out of the darkness and the sudden appearance of the train lifts an explosion of black birds into a deepening sky. Another neck-jerking hour of swaying and rocking, steadying the newspaper and straining into the reflected interior of the windows, another coal-black tunnel sucking the air from the carriage until ear pressure reaches a bursting point and then the flickering of platform, of station and faces as I search for the stiff, grey-haired figure of my grandmother.

She waits in the electric halo of a doorway for me, smiling her aged smile when she locates my wave. Then her powdery hug and wrinkly kiss before we hunch into the sweet leather smell of her Vauxhall, that substandard replacement for Granny May's chauffeured Daimler. I grip the armrest for the short drive to Coates, pressing my foot against an invisible brake pedal and shrinking from the road swerving at me through the windshield as Anthea, another Mr. Toad, careens down narrow Gloucestershire lanes and around blind corners. Often I close my eyes and keep them shut until the sound of the crunching gravel driveway announces our safe arrival at The Thatched House, and then I release the contraction in my shoulders and smile, exhausted, at the sight of the tall leaded windows. While my grandmother parks the car, I step into the thin strip of light escaping from behind the dark window shades and breathe the country air, relieved.

Those weekends are filled with simplicity: shopping at Cirencester market Saturday morning, eating supper in front of the fire, boiled eggs and toast done in "the cooker." Later in the evening I lose to Anthea's surprisingly competitive Scrabble game, my vocabulary no contest for her infinitely larger one. And before bed, we walk into the blinding dark of the Cotswold night, feeling the whiz of bats as they head for the arc of Coates' lone streetlamp. I stand there, under the stars in a sky as black as a magician's cape, listening to the blaze of silence, and wonder at Anthea's capacity to love such remoteness.

Much later, in the bedroom next to my grandmother's, I lie under mounds of wool blankets, willing myself to sleep so I won't have to cross the cold, creaky floor of the landing to use the bathroom. Hours later, still awake, I rise and go to the leaded windowpane, opening it softly, carefully, afraid of the bats that Elizabeth tells me fly in at night, and listen to the piercing quiet.

With my head outside the casement, I know a rush of wisdom like death. The city noise I am used to — horns of trucks en route to market, screaming brakes of non-stop buses and underground trains — has me straining for a sound in that dark night. But here there is only peace, like an alarm.

Early Dreams

*T*he simplicity of a child's rationale is always fascinating. I saw our family group as the perfectly balanced unit — one adult and two children of each sex — and as a child I harboured a strange pride to be from the kind of parents who could arrange such a balance. Obsessed by an early need for order, the fact that there were three of us on each side of the scale, as it were, satisfied my sense of balance.

Eric and Elizabeth provided what many parents in the financial boom of the 1950s had to give: a good home and good opportunities. All we had to do was make good.

The four of us joined the usual groups: after-school Brownie and Scout packs, music and dance lessons or soccer and football teams. From our enclave beyond Vancouver's western boundary, we had no way of seeing that our lifestyle was unusually full. We splashed through the watering of grassy lawns on long summer evenings and crawled through the heart-stopping darkness of the spooky ravine near the beach, completely unaware of a world beyond The Hill. Childhood was a long dance of ignorance, blinded by privilege.

My sister and I shared the largest bedroom in the big house above Burrard Inlet. The northwest view from our corner was the same as the kitchen's below, but without the branches of trees to provide a frame of context. Sitting at our wobbly-legged arborite table, legs swinging above blue linoleum tiles, we rarely noticed the expanse of water, sea and clouds travelling up the Sound and into the cold mountains of the Tantalus Range stretching away from us. Maybe that view was too open, too unenclosed, too much possibility for us to bear.

Elizabeth planned that largest room to be like an English nursery. It was connected to the master bedroom by an accordion door on the other side of their ensuite bathroom. When that was locked — when my father had his bath — the only other way to our mother was down the long dark hallway, past the communal bathroom with its black tiles and pink fixtures; past the adjoining cupboard-sized room where the toilet sat separately and where, if the latch on the sliding door didn't catch, we sometimes burst in on someone in stern concentration; past the closet with its built-in chest of drawers whose cutaway pulls doubled as footholds to the dim electric shadows of the attic above, where ranks of lead soldiers and an electric train set were off-limits to girls and where, whenever possible, my sister and I played on pain of a beating if caught by our brothers; past all these tight rooms of memory to the other bedrooms and the rest of the house where the world was lighter.

My brothers had their own rooms. Charlie lived above the carport in a room filled with shelves and desks, and Chris had a smaller, robin's-egg blue room with a small balcony on the northwest corner. In the early days after moving into the house, Eric and Elizabeth spent weeks laying out the brick patio and landscaping the huge slice of hillside property, filling and emptying their small green wheelbarrow with tons of topsoil. On weekends in those first months, we often ate dinners of peanut butter sandwiches before they put us to bed, planting and cajoling us to sleep like the traumatized bushes and shrubs so recently buried in the garden. They put in cedar hedging and roses, rhododendrons and forsythia, and Elizabeth planted honeysuckle to twist and roll over the wrought-iron railing of the blue room's balcony.

In later years, after Chris had gone, the blue room was the prize my sister and I fought over, lusting after its romantic balcony and the summer scent of honeysuckle wafting in the open glass door.

We lost Chris early. I was 11, the plump curves of puberty just beginning to pull at my chubby body, when his adolescence first thundered through the house. One night Chris argued with my father, and when he slammed out the door, banished for nonconformity, he hurled a rock or a bottle — something hard with loud edges — through the showcase of glass by the front door, his last word on the subject of their disagreement. He was not yet 16.

Eric ran into the dark night after his youngest son, and a nameless fear settled on my mother, my sister and me, waiting inside the house. For the next 15 years the garden outside continued to grow, vivid and green, in spite of the troubles inside.

After his abrupt departure, Chris' name was only mentioned with a kind of strain. His temper and my father's were too much alike, their pride too similar to work together. The hand of time hung over us, waiting.

Elizabeth remembers how the nuns at the Toronto hospital where Chris was born held her legs together to try and delay my brother's arrival before the obstetrician's. She remembers also the lack of social services for parents needing help with special children. In school, Chris' teachers said he wasn't paying attention, and later on, the family counsellor said Eric and Elizabeth weren't paying attention.

We learned to live with the tension of not knowing when or from where Chris would phone, wanting money or a brief respite from life outside, and how Eric would react to each new request. Sometimes the two of them met curtly but with an obvious attempt at improved civility and we'd hold our breath, listening to their exchange from the doorway of the next room. Time after time, the attempted reconciliation would end on terse notes, the strain of effort too much for either one, the edge of the unburied hatchet still too lethal.

Chris always phoned before Christmas. His birthday on the 27th of December meant he could touch my mother for a healthy cheque and a big feed.

December 1976: Elizabeth is nervous, edgy when first the 25th and then the 27th pass without contact. Two or three boxes, wrapped in gay reds and greens, wait under the tree for the delinquent Chris.

"He said he'd come. It's not like him to say he's coming and not show up for Christmas. I'm worried." A mother's intuition.

We pooh-pooh her paranoia, remind her of the times he's shown up unexpectedly at the last minute or just plain late, insist that he's just screwed up. Again. She grows more anxious as each day of the holiday week passes without contact. On one of those last December nights, cleaning up in the kitchen with my sister, I talk about Elizabeth's fears and wonder what has happened to Chris this time.

"Dad told me he had a phone call from the RCMP today," Bizzy says to me. "They've found a body in Ganges Harbour."

I am warm and fuzzy from a night of wine and don't react to her words.

And even when my father phones a week later, the forensic tests done on the body, the dental charts matched, I can't quite grasp the meaning of his words, the way his voice spills them all over the receiver, beads of mercury skidding away from my grabbing fingers. A death in the family. My family. I try to drift away, but the pain of this once-tough man blubbering on the phone and my husband's eyes watching me from the doorway, already knowing, pull me back.

The thought that I struggle with during that long grey drive into Vancouver, coming down the Squamish Highway on the other side of the sound that I grew up on, cold January waves against the rocks below me and January clouds pressing the rocks above me, is that our family is no longer perfectly balanced.

The hardest thing in the world, my mother tells me after the funeral, is to bury your own child.

When she says that, I can't help but think of the abortion she once admitted to having. One, maybe two years after my sister was born, exhausted by the needs of four children and pregnant again, she drove to Seattle to bury a fifth child in a backstreet clinic.

Sometimes life hands you things that aren't meant to be understood. Because the manner of Chris' death was never determined — because his body had been in the cold waters of Georgia Strait for some six weeks — each of us had to find our own way of closing that chapter of life.

I spent those long, empty days after Chris' funeral wondering if my unborn sibling — the faceless, nameless child my mother never had — would have been a boy or a girl, tipping the scales of balance.

Going Home

Two years after Chris died, Eric and Elizabeth gave up trying. Eric moved into a small apartment and seemed, when we saw him, happy and outgoing, though perhaps exaggeratedly so. As far as I knew, this was the first and only time he had ever cooked and done for himself, entertaining old friends and inviting us to dinner every once in a while. He made the separation look easy, natural.

Elizabeth stayed on at the bungalow the family had moved to after Chris left home. She seemed less sure of herself on her own, symptomatic of a life devoted to and defined by others. She was scared of financial independence, incompetent without someone to argue with and, predominantly, lonely.

In the autumn of that first year alone, Elizabeth planned her annual trip to Coates in hopes of rebuilding a relationship with Anthea, the mother she'd never been close to. And when Anthea found out about Elizabeth's separation, she encouraged her daughter to come for a long visit. Later Elizabeth discovered that Anthea had waltzed about the village announcing the demise of her daughter's marriage with a gleefulness that shocked her friends. But for a turn of fate, Elizabeth might have moved back to England.

When Elizabeth arrived at Coates, Anthea was in bed with a flu that rapidly turned to pneumonia. Within a few days, after reminding Elizabeth of the location of keys, papers and various other instructions, Anthea died.

And the trip that my sister and I had thought would be so good for her, getting away from Vancouver with the time to think and talk to old friends and her mother about her newfound situation, turned to disaster.

Overwhelmed by this new crisis on top of everything else, Elizabeth phoned home in a daze.

I am house-sitting for her when the call comes through. Her small, thin voice at the end of the transatlantic cable is unrecognizable, traumatized.

"Mom? Is everything all right?" Behind me the noisy world of kids, playing outside in the late Vancouver summer, explodes. I have to shut my eyes to hear her, listening closely, carefully, to the tinny voice coming from the other side of the world, knowing instinctively that something is wrong.

None of us want to tell Eric about our grandmother's death until after the funeral, knowing, also instinctively, that he will insist on being there. We fly hurriedly to England, leaving jobs and children in chaos to be with our mother through this difficult time. The week unfolds in a sequence of bizarre events, like a Punchinello show.

I go with brother Charles to view Anthea's body, flinch when I see her grinning like the Cheshire cat, her false teeth improperly positioned.

"She looks good, don't you think?" the mortician says confidently, smiling at us patronizingly, and I wince, avoid any response, let Charlie answer him. I come away from the small, grim mortuary unsatisfied.

"It wasn't her," I tell my sister, who didn't want to see the corpse. She shivers, unbelieving.

At the crematorium, still fuzzy with jet lag and time-zone changes, we stare zombie-eyed at the draped coffin on a ledge at the front of the chapel. Alternately pressing close to each other and wiping away refined tears, we pay dismal attention to the service. At the end of the short ritual, a distinct hum interrupts the last line of prayer. The minister invites us to stand, sing one more hymn for our dearly departed, and the organ bursts into trembling chords. On this cue, the quiet pine box in front lurches forward, a temperamental steed, creeping ominously toward two dark drapes fluttering at the end of a hidden track. I turn to my mother, horrified by the realization of a subterranean conveyor belt carrying my grandmother off to God-knows-where, afraid Elizabeth will faint from the trauma of this new shock, but she is hidden in her handkerchief, does not watch the disappearing act.

I listen for the heavy thunk of the coffin as it passes beyond the black curtains, releasing life in a descent through space and time. The crashing finale of the organ floods over me and I hear nothing more than I should. But for weeks after the ceremony, I am plagued by a persistent image of Anthea's horror at such a remarkably tasteless spectacle.

At Coates Church, the 13th-century building across the Common from The Thatched House, we hold a memorial service for the matriarch of our clan. At the front of the church, my brother, delivering the eulogy, chokes on emotions that trip him up and catch at his words; in the front pew, we three women sink into helplessness, numbed by the blatant show of tears on a usually dull man. He declines to ride with us afterwards and instead walks home alone. The emotions of death, like the emotions of life, sit too heavy in the family gullet, and none of us feel able to talk about the tightrope of needs within.

Later, at the tiny grave where Anthea's wooden urn will rest, the family group stands close against the autumn wind. We watch as the rector, that rare friend of Anthea's, places her remains in their final bed, alongside sister Molly. From the dark chasm beside the fresh mound of Cotswold earth, the engraved brass plaque stares up at us and then it is over, the words finished and the flowers thrown. Time to go home.

In the few short days before leaving, though, I feel a gnawing anxiety for the disappearance of my grandmother's lifestyle. Unless I can remember it for her, for all of us, the sands of time will erase any memory of that past way of life. I tell my mother that I would like to see the manor house, go inside and walk through it. After I have nagged sufficiently, she makes a phone call and clears the visit with the caretaker of the Royal Agricultural College, present owner of Coates Manor and its surrounding farmlands.

But she refuses to go with me. "I don't want to see it now," she says.

Thus I walk the narrow country lane alone, heading for the tall stone gateposts outside Coates Manor, its huge iron gates now permanently open, rusted in place. Inside that boundary, I move through the shade of elms planted last century, some as tall as Clayoquot cedars, following their shadows up the gravelled drive. The road winds ahead of me, curving to the left, and I force myself not to run, trying to enjoy my walk but nervous with anticipation, my thoughts racing ahead of my craning neck, trying to see the house at the end of the treed avenue.

On one side of the drive, sunlight reaches through a copse of beech and larch, touching my shoulders and transforming the dappled woods and countryside into a scene from a Turner painting. On the other side, a plowed field ripples away from me toward the Cotswold hills lying scalloped against the horizon like the back of a great dragon, though gentler and without the scales.

Just beyond the curve I come to a wooden gate, also left open, hanging from its last intact hinge. Ahead, I think to myself, I will see the flowers: irises, roses, hollyhocks, larkspur, all arranged in their segregated beds of whites, yellows, blues, pinks. And on the right, I remember from all the photos, will be the pond with its buried brass lamps and oil paintings. I smile, wondering if a glint of metal or the white of Thomas Firth's eye — the in-law whose dark portrait was banished here as "No great loss to the nation" — will peer up at me when I stand at the murky edge of the pond.

But when I turn the corner, it isn't like that at all and I have to pretend.

I have not, until now, understood the size of Coates Manor. Standing in the middle of the gravel sweep before the main entrance, my mood of bubbling expectancy is silenced by the hugeness of the pillars, the shrinking I feel before this enormous symbol of the past. All my thoughts, all my memories of stories from another time, are focussed now on this grand mausoleum.

After several moments of stunned reaction, I step toward and up the stairs to the massive front doors, push daintily against their solidity until I realize my entire body weight is required to open them.

Inside, large squares of black and white marble spread lavishly before a glazed door that opens into a reception hall. The vastness of the hall and the ornate plasterwork on the ceiling sit imperiously before me, and I wonder whether they don't belong more to an Italian palace than this quiet country manor. A carved mahogany banister, the likes of which I've previously only seen in federal buildings or university libraries, rises imposingly from the centre of the hall, as austere and commanding as the Lady of the Lake. At the other end of the hall, beside several dark, closed doors, a huge marble fireplace adorned with more carved plaster stretches from floor to ceiling like some kind of icon. Here, I remember, tea was served in front of the roaring flames punctually at 4:30.

The closed doors lead from the hall into the far reaches of the main floor. One, I know, will take me to the back regions and servants' quarters, another to the underground wine cellars, and one to something called the flower room, which housed the only telephone in the manor while Granny May was alive. Through several archways, and beneath more ceiling friezes, oversized wooden doors lead into the billiard, music and drawing rooms, and from there into the library. The library is the coziest room on the main floor, a smaller 23-foot room instead of the 40-foot length of the other reception rooms. In here, Granny May drew her armchair close to the small English fireplace, sitting beneath the framed silhouettes of ancient relatives on the walls and surrounded by floor-to-ceiling shelves of leather-bound books. The drawing room, which would have been the usual place for entertaining guests, was used only whenever non-family arrived, and then the Sienna marble mantel with its delicately carved nudes and scrolled sconces would glow with the flames of a more sedate fire.

But when I wander in and out of these rooms, they are dull, miserable, barren of any past or present life. The furniture, when there is any, is bland and institutional, predominated by the likes of folding metal chairs and student-scarred tables. I have to close my eyes to picture the great expanse of Indian broadloom in the music room, the polished wainscotting in the billiards room, the grandfather clock that I remember placed just so in the photos of the drawing room. In and out of the great double-width doors I wander, and finally my eyes, wearied by the inside devastation, lean toward the view outside. Beyond the leaded bay window in the library I can see the Roman-built Fosse Way far across the park and I wonder if the eyes of the ancient governor Gaius are upon me now, sympathetic and nostalgic. This must be how he felt when, in the first century, so much of the work he had to abandon was left to disintegrate, unappreciated, misunderstood.

I float up the stairs feeling ghostlike, not at all grounded, trying to assess the feel of this place, the seat of ancestors whose forgotten lives are buried behind these unpainted walls grubby with fingerprints and scuffs. I walk down the uncarpeted hallway that replays my empty footsteps and peek into unfurnished rooms with peeling walls, the plaster in need of repair or paint, usually both. And when I turn a corner and come upon a large room at the back of the house, its windows looking over an empty, rut-filled paddock, I realize I have found Elizabeth's old nursery.

The sound of a child calls to me across time, then, feet clapping on the wooden floors in this large, barren room, and my eyes imagine a fire in the blue-and-white Delft-tiled hearth, an old woman sewing in a rocking chair while the child's voice fills this house of empty rooms. Standing there among the ruins, I am filled with an unnameable ache: I want to salvage something of that dramatic era from my past, something tangible that connects me to an extinct time. It's important, for some indecipherable reason, to claim my English birthright without relinquishing my other, wilderness roots.

On my desk sits a piece of Delft tile — a blue swan sliding in front of a blue willow — rescued from the crumbling mortar of Elizabeth's nursery fireplace, carefully pried so as not to add to the rubble of breakage already accumulated on the hearth. And from one of the manor bathrooms, where a ball-footed tub sat amidst an expanse of shattered slate, smashed when the gravity of heavy brass bore down upon it, I picked up a tarnished coat hook. I wouldn't normally have taken it without asking — though who would I have asked? — but when I glanced at the walls, frowning to comprehend how the hook had arrived on the floor, I felt a spark of molten rage low in my gut.

Splinters of wood jutting from the back of the door announced a wound where once the brass hook had been mounted. The realization that the hook had been wrenched from the wooden flesh by gleeful, destructive hands, hands whose owners knew more about cow manure and crop sowing than good manners or respect, made me splutter in anger. I turned to go, saw where the plaster walls had been kicked in by some other irreverent limb, an appendage without connections or sympathy to an earlier time in this house, and I understood more clearly than my mother or grandmother could ever have taught me why I needed to salvage something of their lost world.

I had the idea, then, of bringing home a part of my history. As if a piece of the manor was something to rebuild from, a place to begin again. I gathered those two pieces of my past, the Delft tile and brass hook, hid them beneath my sweater and ran down the stairs clutching them to my belly like a childless woman kidnapping a baby from a supermarket buggy. And as I hunched down the long gravel drive, heart thumping conspicuously, I struggled against the tears that welled up without warning, startling me into thoughts of loss and ownership, class and status. It is the old internal argument about who I am; upper class or working class, white collar or blue. My shame, my pride.

I don't tell my mother about the items I've removed from Coates Manor, but hide them at the bottom of my suitcase. Then Charlie and I begin the long trek back to B.C., saying goodbye to Bizzy and her infant son staying on with Elizabeth. On the train to Heathrow, I am squeezed empty of emotion as the green hills and farm fields dwindle, then disappear, transplanted by soot-encrusted brick buildings. At Heathrow, I swallow travel-sickness pills to help me sleep through the dead hours of flying, trying to sever myself from this land where now my grandmother's seeds are discarded and forgotten, her life eaten by history and time.

When I wake hours later, drained and stiffened, we are swooping over the Fraser River delta, the North Shore mountains banked behind a dipping silver wing. In that moment, the rawness of Canada's evergreens, rivers and oceans fills me with a bursting sense of release, even though in my mind I still picture the quiet hills of the English west country.

Survival of the Species

*A*nthea's obsession with quiet eventually drove my parents to search for a separate residence in which to stay during their visits to Coates. Being able to maintain her own privacy as well as have Elizabeth close at hand appealed to Anthea so much that she decided to donate a piece of land for my parents to build on. Lying close to The Thatched House, the property sidled up to its extremities but remained separated by an old orchard. Anthea could walk through the hedge at the far end of her garden and peer over the fence next to the large south field to watch the construction, and while the building was in progress, she'd do this daily, reporting via letters as the land was cleared and the foundations poured for the small house to be called Beech Cottage.

Today the garden is grown and the cottage stands in the stillness of its Cotswolds grove, a home away from home for the daughter and son-in-law who wanted to be near but not at The Thatched House while visiting Anthea. Beech Cottage is another of Anthea's legacies to us, but one that embodies something more than an inheritance. The peace with which Anthea strove to cocoon herself is still there, a haven in the restful surroundings of my grandmother's country.

The view from Beech Cottage is the same one my grandmother once admired from her drawing room in The Thatched House. I see her, standing in the big bay window, old grey eyes embracing the distant green, steadied by the comfort of the Gloucestershire hills.

And years later, when I introduce my daughter to the Cotswolds, it is with a gentle pride in those hills undulating through my past and her future.

When Eric and Elizabeth built Beech Cottage, they included some North American touches: an open living area and a shower stall in the second bathroom, as well as a more accommodating version of the traditionally small English hearth. And as a final embellishment to the construction, they placed a limestone plaque over the door of the little house:

E. & E. B.

1979

Before the house was finished, though, Anthea had died and Eric and Elizabeth had separated. In 1980, after burying my grandmother, Bizzy and I stood with Elizabeth beneath the plaque and stared at the carved letters.

"It'll have to come out, I guess," Elizabeth said.

My sister and I nodded dully, not sure how to respond to that half-question, half-statement. Opening the door to this house for the first time, standing under the oak-beamed ceilings inside, I wondered why the stone had been placed at all, separation being so inevitable. And yet somehow it looked just fine above the mullioned doorway. It belonged.

Beech Cottage was named for the two other Beech Cottages that preceded it. The first was a playhouse for Anthea and Molly, built on the grounds of their childhood home at Norton Hall. I forget, though, until I come across a picture of the two girls beside the playhouse — an early photograph in brown and ivory shades of button boots and bonnets, full skirts and pinafores — that the original Beech Cottage was built of wood and not the usual limestone of the Cotswolds.

The Cotswold District Council is the authority that permits buildings to be erected or changed in the county of Gloucestershire.

New construction must conform to a style of architecture inherent to the west country, buildings made of the local limestone quarried there since earliest history.

To an unappreciative eye, the weathered stone is a dull grey-brown, as drab and uninspiring as dust. First-time tourists to the Cotswolds are apt to be unimpressed by the plainness of the architecture, and without a personal tour through the unknown villages, there would be only the memory of having once visited this distant part of the world. But lost in old valleys as deep as the Fraser Canyon there are endless details which once Anthea and now Elizabeth points out for tourists: old mullioned windows and Roman ruins on stumbling hillsides, the stone cross of an ancient Celtic marketplace or a Shakespearean-era house. After driving the narrow country roads with my mother, I come away with a familiarity and a sense of belonging as big as my native land.

And it is this continual pulling at my centre by two different extremes that has me struggling to find a home on one side of the Atlantic or the other. Incongruous images are etched in my DNA, simultaneously dear and familiar: the soft-coloured woodcuts of dress-coated soldiers and plump, red-cheeked milkmaids beside the desolate hues of Toni Onley's northern coastlines or Emily Carr's raven in a vivid green forest.

Elizabeth's childhood playhouse, the second Beech Cottage, snuggles into a small clearing just east of The Thatched House. Here, sheltered by a copse of tall evergreens and nestled between the fenced field and a neighbouring house, my sister and I re-enacted our English heritage. In the early 1960s, we two unkempt Canadians used to the non-restrictions of vacant lots for playgrounds followed Anthea into the copse outside the house and watched, big-eyed, as she unlocked the playhouse door with a set of large, iron keys.

Day after day then, Bizzy and I presided over our own manor house, clearing it of cobwebs, beetles and the remains of several small animals, setting the furniture just so, readying our residence for a new life. From my reluctant grandmother we wheedled props, running excitedly to and from The Thatched House with armloads of candle stubs, tea sets, shawls, handkerchiefs — materials to help us relive the history of our strange English relatives, drawing on the stories that simultaneously petrified and excited us, making sleep in an old English house impossible. We dramatized the haunted dining room at Clifton Maubank where the chairs mysteriously pulled away from the table precisely at 8:00 PM, and the bedroom of young Mary Lewton's cousin where an old man, in a 17th-century velvet evening coat, lace front and cuffs, wearing a nightcap and carrying a candlestick, leaned over her bed in the middle of the night. And later, the room in a Yorkshire boarding house where May went as a young bride on holiday and woke to find an old woman rocking in a chair at the foot of her bed, apron flung over her head as she wept.

⌒⌒⌒

When I am 17, down from London on one of those weekend visits to my grandmother, I walk into the woods to revisit the small playhouse, smiling when I see the miniature Dutch door that I'd forgotten 'til then. Inside are two miniature Windsor chairs and a gateleg table, copies of furniture in The Thatched House, beside them the wooden cradle that once held an imaginary baby. The large cooking hook, swung out over the hearth where we must have left it last, still holding the wrought-iron pot stirred so seriously by Bizzy or me, empty now. I put out my shoe, tap at the wing-sided rocker and listen to the quiet grating sound on the concrete floor, remembering. The playhouse is small and dark now, quiet with so many years of disuse. When I turn to leave, I shut the door on those cobwebs of memory, such small dark moments that make up our lives.

And the carved stone above the door of the third Beech Cottage is still in place, greying with age, its engraved letters dusted now with a faint blanket of lichen.

⌒⌒⌒

"When did it get hard for you?" I ask Elizabeth quietly, knowing the difficulty of this subject for her. I am touching on the separation of my parents when they were 50 and 51 years old.

"Hard one to answer." Her voice is very faint. "I think it was never easy."

"Why did you never go home, back to England?" I'm asking what's different about her from me. Why did she suffer through the hard times, refuse to give up?

"I *couldn't* go home. For one thing, I hadn't any money, and for another, I don't think I would have felt welcome. And I guess it was pride, too. I didn't want to give my family the chance to say, 'We told you so.'"

I'm watching her face, trying to judge how many of these reasons have to do with fear. I remember Anthea's fierce moods, remember how easily they frightened the bravest of souls.

"But do you remember how ..." I hesitate, looking for the right word, "relieved your mom was when she heard you had separated?" Anthea had never told Elizabeth she missed her, never asked her to come home to live, never talked about the abandonment she felt when her daughter emigrated, but when she heard that Eric and Elizabeth had split, she was elated. "Do you think, now, it would have been okay to go home earlier?" It's not a fair question, I know, because what I am really asking is why Elizabeth didn't bring me up to be English instead of Canadian, but I seem to need this information from her.

"I suppose it would. It never entered my head, though." Elizabeth looks at me then, to make sure I'm paying close attention when she adds, "And I guess we really, seriously — I'm not joking — did belong to a generation that thought you jolly well fight it out somehow. You make it stick."

She is talking about her marriage and about her children's marriages, about all marriages. As she speaks, the numbing memories recur: the slow decay of a relationship and the way it lingers like a malicious nausea. And then, as if to pull me down further, I remember nights in that childhood bedroom at the big house, listening to the stab of loud voices coming through the floor from downstairs as my sister and I lay in bed, even the corners of our room harbouring toughness.

"And I suppose I was stubborn because my parents were divorced and I'd always resented that," she continues. I am uncomfortable hearing Elizabeth defend her choices, as if she were on trial, as if I put her there. "I was determined my children weren't going to grow up in a broken home, but actually in many ways it was a very debatable point ..." Her voice trails off and she frowns as she thinks about that statement. I wait and she starts over.

"And again, I guess I always felt that because of his leg I had to go that extra mile because he ..." I squirm with the fullness of her pause, wanting to change the topic but aware the discussion is somehow therapeutic. "... because he had more to contend with than most people. Perhaps." She adds that last word with heavy doubt, as if here — now — she's unsure of even that fact.

I am feeling exposed, hearing this confession, as if I'm guilty of knowing things I shouldn't.

"It would have been *easier* to have left somebody who hadn't had a very bad injury like that," she adds. The finality of those words feels harsh, judgmental.

"You felt responsible in a lot of ways?"

"No, not responsible, but just that ... it would not be a very nice thing to do." Her shoulders sag a little and she grows sorrowful, recognizing, perhaps, that things could have been different. "I don't know. I suppose if I'd had the sort of home where I knew I'd get a really wonderful, warm welcome, I probably would have cleared out, yes."

I think how easy it has always been — perhaps too easy — for me to go home to my parents, to ask for help and know it will be given. When I become an orphan, will I be as capable on my own as Elizabeth has had to be?

In 1983, Eric and Elizabeth decided to try again, resurrect their disintegrated partnership. For many years afterwards they took up residence at Coates each fall, working on the garden and Beech Cottage, cleaning and repairing old dark memories.

Prehistoric Millstones

*E*very four or five years I decide I'm not at home in my current residence and I fidget with thoughts of moving. A home must contain me as much as my grandmother's furniture, though, and sometimes I have felt trapped, bound by those heirlooms as much as my heritage. My last two homes were both chosen for their west-coast ambience, one a post-and-beam with lots of glass and tongue-in-groove cedar, and the other a small waterfront cottage at the edge of Georgia Strait. But more important than their environmental appeal was their ability to accommodate my ten-foot-tall grandfather clock with its rotating faces of the moon.

The 19th-century footbath filled with African violets, the Victorian parlour suite upholstered in pink silk brocade, the dainty Welsh sideboard whose inlay regularly peels itself off in the centrally heated homes of North America — all of these were given me when my grandmother died. I was 28 at the time, unaware of a need for roots and naïve about the difference in value between my eclectic mix of furniture and the valuable effects of my grandmother's life.

⤳

A container of furniture was shipped from England via the Panama Canal after Anthea died. During the four months that we waited for the freighter to arrive, the shoddy furnishings of my youth were discarded with the scorn of the nouveau riche. A "desk" made from an old door covered in gold-flecked turquoise arborite, with wrought-iron legs that wobbled because the screws were always coming loose — the very same table that had sat in front of the panoramic windows of my childhood bedroom where my sister and I cut out paper dolls and glued pictures from magazines onto Mother's Day cards or performed complicated operations on various dolls — this historic piece was heaved irreverently onto the trailer destined for the dump. The waterfall walnut dressing table, sawn in half by my father and refinished into two nightstands for the master bedroom, its large round mirror donated to the rec-room wall where it was trimmed, over the years, with coasters and matchbooks from the many bars and nightclubs my parents visited on foreign holidays; the worn, sagging armchairs with knobbly 1950s upholstery destroyed by cat claws and roughhousing children; pole lamps of incredible ugliness — all were removed in preparation for having "real" furniture.

The 16-wheeler that steamed up the quiet suburban street with an ordinary plank container on its back heralded our new beginnings. The wooden box sat on our parents' front lawn like a huge pine coffin while we danced around it, squealing at the driver to hurry with his crowbar. A time of anticipation, a time of anxiety.

The first crack of splitting wood drew a yell of excitement. Bizzy and I burrowed into the wood shavings, pulling and pushing, feeling for the hard shape of something familiar. When the first treasure was exhumed, stray whiskers of packing material clinging to polished wood, a sharp odour accompanied it. It was the scent of my grandmother's home, wafting out of the dark packing box and tugging at my nose, pushing me down the hallways of memory.

The Thatched House smelled of something associated with oldness, history, better times. In the front hall, walking from the library to the drawing room on a flagstoned floor framed by a sheen of woods — oak wainscotting, walnut sideboard and mahogany clock — a smell that blended furniture polish, damp wood and musk always stopped me. I never walked through the glass front doors without noticing that sharp scent, its pungence a sort of uncomfortable pleasure.

And later, standing on a lawn halfway round the world from the quarried limestone of The Thatched House, smelling that familiar mustiness under the glare of summer and trees, I felt removed from this present incarnation. The smell, more than the furniture itself, connected me to another world in ways I cannot fully explain. My grandmother's country, my second home, contains the roots of my prehistoric — pre-Canadian — nature.

Items rescued from the dark interior of the shipping container that day brought shouts of memories: "It's the cane collection from the box room!" "Here's the china lady that sat on Granny's desk!" Our initial hysteria gradually slipped into a mood of determined silence as more and more of our grandmother was unearthed. The exhumation took all afternoon, and at the end of it we sat, surrounded by our English legacy.

For days I wandered in and out of the house smelling the oldness, holding on to that proof of my heritage and the belief in another life. After a point, the smell became like so many other things from my grandmother's world — misplaced, unidentifiable, disappeared.

Sometimes now, when I'm alone, I sit in the living room and listen to the dull, flat sound of the grandfather clock marking the passage of time. I try to imagine the many exotic places this 200-and-some-year-old clock has inhabited and wonder if the fir-shrouded hillsides of the Pacific Northwest aren't the strangest of all those homes.

But the antiques from my grandmother's house, the old pieces that were my grandmother and which I loved because they were so much a part of her, have now become a burden. I carry them like millstones, worrying about new breakage whenever I move, ashamed that I do not — as my grandmother's housekeeper did — polish them weekly. I hover nearby whenever teenagers are about, youths who kick or lean indiscriminately, and pass coasters to people who put damp containers on the cracked, old woods without thinking.

In a repetitive dream, I redecorate my west-coast home with the Sante Fe look, clean simple lines, no brass, no ornate inlay or moulding. Just furniture with a function.

But of course this oldness is my history, the hardest part of life to forget.

In 1993 that history comes to the fore.

Under a hot September sun, Eric and Elizabeth dance to the soft music of Glenn Miller's "String of Pearls." They move easily across the small deck of a yacht, careful not to jar old joints, so fragile now. From the railing at the side of the deck, I admire their synchronicity, their intuitive movements with each other, and wonder when that stopped between them.

In the background, above the faces of old friends watching with me as these two step and turn, arms out and hands entwined, are the dark mountainsides, darker waters of Indian Arm. The heat of this late-fall day is a surprise to many of us, here to celebrate Eric and Elizabeth's golden wedding anniversary.

The afternoon slides away, consumed by moments of talking, laughing, eating, listening, drinking — moments that spread out, join into one another, frames in a movie that I'll play back in my mind for many nights to come. We snap photos, posing familiar old faces to save, collect in more albums of memories for other generations.

Lured onto the boat under pretense of planning for a future celebration, Elizabeth is not as dressed up as she would like to be, but while they dance, it's hard to see beyond her pleasure.

We lift glasses of cool wine in the bright heat of September, drink a toast to the golden couple, and Eric, overcome by emotion, surprises us with tears. To lighten the moment, the toastmaster makes jokes.

"Because Eric had only one leg, it was easier for Elizabeth to catch him." We titter while Elizabeth feigns shock, shakes her finger at the old friend. Hard memories handled with humour.

In another speech, my brother refers to the drab rationings of most wartime weddings: "Because meat was a scarcity, whale became, for obvious reasons, the most available source of meat. And they ate so much whale that they even made up a song about it: 'Whale meet

214

again, don't know where, don't know when …'" His purposely out-of-tune voice fades into the applause and laughter.

At the end of the day, clasping hands and saying goodbye to all the old faces, adults who once danced in the rec room of that big house on the Endowment Lands, shared tables and umbrellas at church picnics and school sports days, traded boats for cabins and watched us grow up as we watched them grow old, I am content with the success of the party but disheartened by the failure of life. I watch the old folks as one by one they ease themselves off the boat, tottering onto the gangplank and along the dock, hard of hearing or hard of sight, often both, white-haired and slow. I have to bite my lip against the cry that hovers there: "Come back!"

"I know you won't believe this," my mother tells me, "but this has been the happiest day of my life. It's like the wedding we never had." I hug her goodbye, wondering why she thinks I couldn't believe that.

When we leave the boat, thanking the white-uniformed and gold-braided captain, I try not to notice his impatience to get home, end today's long, hot job.

~~><

I used to think my daughter was the only one I knew who didn't want to grow up, grow older. This business of fighting with life — I've become so good at it that I'm hardly aware of its presence — is not a skill I can harness. Now I sense a need to release the past, to move forward.

Final Regrets

"Why do you want to say things like that about your family?" Elizabeth worries aloud.

"It's what I remember, Mother, not necessarily the truth."

"But you can't send that to a publisher, dear."

"Why?"

"Because you wouldn't want people to think that's really the way we are."

It doesn't matter how often I try to explain art and life and the writer's vision, Elizabeth is reserved about this work. She struggles with the question of why, if she was a good mother, her daughter draws unflattering pictures of the family. My words on paper are a betrayal; they will linger after her memory and taint the family history. Surely this daughter is not the same one whose blonde hair she plaited so many decades ago, the girl whose school awards nights she witnessed with so much pride? She says none of this, but the thoughts pass visibly over her face, tired with time.

Across the table from me are two people whose lives I have lived while reading and writing about them. Now I am confused about who they are.

The old man in front of me concentrates on methodically scraping the sides of his cereal bowl, collecting stray threads of Shredded Wheat and patting them into a puddle of mush before digging his spoon into the smooth surface. He bends his head, pushes his tongue forward in a kind of greeting and squeezes his eyelids shut as the spoon lifts toward his mouth. The precision of his actions during this morning routine fascinates me.

They are elderly people, Eric and Elizabeth, though neither has considered this possibility. Eric, in particular, has a pouchy and swollen face, a crown of white above his ears, an overgrown beard in need of grooming. I think of how far removed they are from those photos in my office, those haunting images of youth preserved in celluloid, a camouflage of black and white.

Eric likes to give the impression that he was once very respected, despite middle-class beginnings, by fellow lawyers and other business acquaintances. He gives me a professional law journal to read, yellow post-it notes marking pages that celebrate other graduates from that UBC class of 1948. Does he attach himself to some part of their fame? He speaks with glowing eyes about his beginnings as a young criminal lawyer, working with so-and-so, now a Supreme Court judge or Queen's Counsel, levels of the profession that he would have liked to reach. I hear his unspoken sense of failure, but I don't question his need for embellishments; they are the only way to maintain a waning zeal for life, a life that hasn't been what it could have.

Now he talks about his mother again, how lovely she was.

"Do you remember her well, Dad?" I'm still looking for something to redeem his lost ancestors, especially the harsh-looking Eileen.

He doesn't look at me when he answers. He stares out the window at the branches of Douglas firs dancing beneath the weight of squirrels and blue jays fighting for seeds.

"Oh yes, a wonderful woman. And pretty? You've never seen anything like it! There's a big picture in there." He points at a black scrapbook on the table in front of us. "You'll see. I'd like a copy of it, blown up, for my wall."

He never says "please," this man, always assumes he can have what he wants without the usual niceties. And I feed his presumptive manner.

"Okay, Pop," I nod, opening the book to look for the photo he refers to. On the first page, though, is the mesmerizing photo of Eric and Elizabeth's reunion kiss, that moment of forgotten passion, and once again I am stunned by the obvious blatancy of their ardour. But because I am in front of my father, a man who lost the ability to be familiar all those years ago, the intimacy in the photo makes me uncomfortable. I slide my eyes past the embrace of the young couple, concentrate instead on the vertical seams in the riveted metal behind them, the side of the train car from which Elizabeth has so recently stepped before pressing close to Eric.

This is the Vancouver meeting with the throng of Browns and a mother-in-law who brought a reporter to capture her son's image for the society page. And Eric's crutches, pinned by his reaching arms, a strong reminder of the hard work ahead.

"What about this photo, Dad? Wouldn't you like a blow-up of this one?" I hold the album up to show him their reunion kiss, trying to rekindle something else.

"What for? I can look at your mother any day of the week!"

His scornfulness betrays me. I turn away quickly, glance at the other photos on the page, yellowed clippings of Vancouver boys maimed by the war, gone missing, presumed dead. Turning another page I see Eric's stern brow, early camouflage for youth and fear, on the wing of the huge Halifax, flanked by the crew that relied on him, young men with cocky ideas about fixing Jerry and righting the world. And the aircraft, like the enemy sky, so large it dwarfs them.

"Or this one?" I hold up the young men smiling at the camera with innocent naiveté.

"No. Just the one of my mother."

He is not looking at me and his annoyance is audible. I stare at his profile thinking how Elizabeth must often feel as I do now, bursting to yell at his curt dismissal. The room fills with the pressure of my silent grief and I choke on the hard feelings rising in my gullet. There is a closeness of denial in this strangled room, but instead of answering his hardness I roll my eyes at the wall.

One-half of my background sits before me in the body of this man. Galloping through my veins, tying me to him in a way I can't discard, are the genetic records of his past, my heritage, a connection too strong to abandon. When I sit at his hospital bedside some day in the future, hold a swollen blue hand and regret his harsh ways, this man's life will be my connection through time to a forgotten history. And his unbecoming nature, so unlike the gentle fathers in childhood books, *Dick and Jane* and *Nancy Drew*, is the price of this relationship.

I push on, find another photo, unwilling to give up trying.

"Where's this, Pop?"

Royal Alexandra Hotel say the words on the rotting marquis, sagging in the middle so that the "l" of *Royal* and the "A" in *Alexandra* tip dangerously forward, tempted overboard by age or disrepair.

Eric's bushy white eyebrows raise themselves up until the blue eyes beneath them look as if they can actually see again, but he shakes his old head.

"I don't know, dear. I really don't know."

What point is served by keeping things — photos, books, furniture, paintings — if the inheritor is unable to identify and immortalize them? Eric requires only the photos of his mother to connect with the past, leaving me with nothing more than filtered DNA to dissect and explore for the source of my Brown-ness. Some family traits I can attribute to his Irish blood and the red-haired temperament of a great-great-grandfather from County Armagh, but Eric's foremothers — Marianne Atchison, Sarah Bates, Jane Hill — are ghosts for whom I can only imagine stories, and so I conjure miserable marriages to demanding, dictatorial husbands, the hardness of those early days in a harsh new country.

When I bring up the subject of those early women on the Canadian side of the family, Elizabeth snorts. "Only *that* kind of women came out to Canada on their own." When I look at her uncomprehendingly, she continues: "Prisoners, prostitutes." She waits for my look of understanding, and then her tone softens. "I guess so many of them were mail-order brides, women with not much future. It was a pretty sad gamble for most of them, but maybe it was better than what they had back home."

All those blank faces, all those lost stories trapped in the photograph albums of sons like Eric who can't remember them. I stare at the names written longhand inside the cover of Eileen's family Bible, try to touch them into life using only my imagination for a wand, but they will only lie there dead.

Their stories must be built from the framework of living personalities, those diluted remnants of forgotten ancestors. And with so many years of subtle training behind me, of being taught that the English branches of my family, with its loftier heights and sturdier roots, are somehow superior, I have blamed the family shortcomings and personal foibles on these rougher, Canadian ancestors.

But the English side also troubles me in a way I would never have predicted. Sometimes, now, I wear my grandmother's diamonds with an uncomfortable feeling of posturing. In the presence of some — those who scorn, or envy, the ostentations and wealth of the elite — I turn the ring until the diamonds cut into the skin of my palm and only the gold band is visible on the back of my hand. This wealth is not me, that action says — only my past.

And now that past is fading, disappearing with the remains of a disintegrating family. The two opposing branches of relatives still cannot be meshed in any kind of acceptable union. At this last, I see my job is not to join, but to remember.

"Thanks for the scrapbook, Dad," I say when I leave. "I'll look through it later."

The large book with its several loose pages, edges frayed and torn, comes home with me and lies on the stairs, ignored even when my eye or foot happens on its blackness waiting there. Several weeks later I lift the album and carry it to my office, open it to search the faces of relatives already forgotten by Eric and to look for the picture that inspired his canonization of Eileen. Finding nothing new, I turn back to the beginning, back to the picture of my young parents at the train station.

I pick gently at the photo's edges, and when it lifts easily I tack it on the wall above my computer, close the book on the rest.

Epilogue

So Far from Home

Sixteen-year-old Pierre Barré stood at his open bedroom window in the black hours of a late June night. He peered into the darkness, recognizing the shadow of the village hall and puzzling over the noise he could hear out there. When he raised the window further and leaned out to have a better look, what he saw surprised him. In the village square was a gathering of townspeople, their low murmur of voices anxious in the hush of the night. But Pierre could see nothing obvious to alert his suspicion. Then, from somewhere beyond the townspeople, a loud yell rose into the night. Pierre saw the figures in front of the village hall start with fright and then heard again the piercing sound of a voice in distress.

When a third yell rose, Pierre frowned and turned away from the window. He felt his way along the shadowy hallway to his parents' bedroom, knocking softly on their door. Opening it, Pierre spoke quickly to the questioning voice of his father. A few minutes later, back at his own bedroom window, Pierre watched his father moving through the darkened village with his employee, Maurice Gobin. Maurice's dog, Sichy, trotted beside his master, happy to be out on a midnight adventure.

As another yell lifted from the blackness beyond the square, Pierre leans out the window to see his father hurry toward the gathered villagers. Several people turned when the farmer and his helper arrived, their hands lifting in nonverbal gestures as they explained their presence at such a strange hour.

Pierre saw his father listen and then turn to look in the direction of another disembodied yell coming from somewhere beyond the square. With Maurice and the dog, the farmer moved toward the fields skirting the village, and Pierre shivered with fear for his father. Somewhere out there the Germans were on watch.

It seemed a long time before Pierre's father reappeared, this time running and without the company of Maurice. The farmer hurried past the townspeople, calling for help as he headed for the nearest farmhouse, but none of the others moved. The owner of the farmhouse allowed M. Barré to take his travois-like carrier used for the transport of slaughtered pigs, but he too refused to help. Pierre's father dragged the contraption back toward the fields blanketed by the night, passing the gathering in the square once again.

The yells had subsided, Pierre realized, but shortly after his father disappeared again, they recommenced, this time at increased volume. Now the sounds turned to screams of pain, and as Pierre squinted in the direction of the noise, the vague shape of a dog appeared.

Directly behind Sichy, Pierre could just make out his father and Maurice leaning into the poles of the travois, hauling at the weight behind them with difficulty. The townspeople in the square shook their heads gravely as the travois passed, but they remained silent. Pierre heard the raised voice of the mayor telling his father, "It's not a good idea, M. Barré." But the farmer kept at his struggle.

The weight in the travois was a body, Pierre could see, and the body continued to cry out as the farmer and his helper dragged him toward the farmhouse.

Pierre's mother stood beside her son now, hands clutching at the neck of her dressing gown. She shook her head as the effect of her husband's actions began to dawn on her.

"My God!" she whispered.

Pierre, understanding his mother's fear, lifted his eyes and peered behind his father and the village square into the blacker distance beyond. His eyes searched the night, looking for the telltale glint of German armaments in the dark. He looked back at the vision of his father's laboured trek through the village and heard the intense cry of the man behind him on the travois. Farther back, Sichy the dog was now sniffing curiously at the trail of scent left by the person Pierre was hauling.

Pierre followed his mother down the stairs and outside into the courtyard. As his father and Maurice rounded the corner of the drive, it became obvious that the person in the travois was no longer conscious.

"Phone the doctor," M. Barré called to his wife.

"You can't bring that man here!" Mme. Barré argued. "We'll all be taken prisoner if they find him here! Think about the safety of your family, for God's sake, man!"

But the two men continued to heave the travois toward the door. At the threshold of the farmhouse they gently lowered the poles of their burden. Pierre's brother and sister had appeared in the doorway, wakened by the voices, and now someone held up a light to reveal that the injured man was a pilot.

They had heard the bombers overhead and the German guns in the distance, but ever since D-day the noise had been a constant backdrop of daily life. There had been no sudden flames or explosions from planes shot down over the fields, so where had this pilot come from? Now, thanks to Pierre's father, he was here in their house, endangering their lives as much as his own.

The family stood above the pilot in silence. In the beam of the flashlight they noticed his bright red hair, his mangled uniform and the utter horror of his injury. The whole of his right foot was missing, and where the foot should have been was only a bloody mess of bone and flesh. What remained of the right trouser leg was saturated by blood from the open wound.

The pilot moaned and again M. Barré told his wife to call the doctor. She looked up at her husband and opened her mouth to protest, but Paul Barré merely nodded at her. His wife shook her head but turned and went inside.

The children, Pierre included, hovered in the doorway, appalled by the state of the pilot's injury. As farm children they were used to seeing the bloody gore of butchered animals, but had never before been exposed to such an explicit vision of the physical horrors of war. The degree of the pilot's wound terrified Pierre, and he realized with clarity his mother's concern. If this man died in their care, the Germans would hold them to blame. Could they dispose of the body before the Germans found him? What if someone from the village turned them in? It had happened before that the Germans bribed villagers to inform on their neighbours by offering rewards of sugar and coffee. Pierre knew it could happen in his community just as easily as any other. Would he and his siblings still be together tomorrow, or would the Germans have taken them all away? Would any of them ever see their friends again, or would they simply disappear into the blackness of this night?

These thoughts ran through his head as he stared at the wounded soldier. He watched his father and Maurice bend over the pilot now, sliding their arms beneath the injured man to try and lift him from the travois. A scream pierced the air and all three of the children looked away into the dark, shivering with fear.

M. Barré and Maurice Gobin frowned with concern, but after a few moments of discussion they persevered with their efforts, lifting and carrying the howling and terrified officer into the farmhouse. They took him through the entrance hall and down the few stairs into the kitchen, and with each step the pilot bellowed in pain. The children were sent for bandaging and Mme. Barré reappeared to say that the doctor was on his way.

By now the whole family recognized that the wounded man was unlikely to live. When the pilot motioned with his fingers toward his lips, they fed him some wine, but, after a second try, they realized the wine would not stay in his stomach. The aviator continued to heave even after they stopped, and when the doctor arrived from the next village, he was visually shocked by the wretched state of the man. Doctor Barot shook his head in dismay, as if questioning the sense of trying to help this dying man, but gave the pilot an injection to calm his nerves and settle his pain.

"He needs to be in hospital. There's too much blood lost. There is nothing I can do for him," the doctor said from beside the pilot's makeshift bed on the kitchen table. The family stared helplessly at the injured man, fearful of what to do next.

But M. Barré, the man who had sneered at the fear of the other townspeople, was not daunted. He nodded at the doctor and thanked him for coming, then went into the hallway to call the authorities. The official transport arrived quickly and made arrangements for the pilot's removal to the nearest hospital, and as they watched the painful ordeal of moving the Canadian, none of the Barrés believed that Eric would survive the night. All of them, including Pierre, felt that the effort to save the foreigner may have only endangered the family.

Fifty-six years later, reading through the mail saved for him while he and his wife were away on holiday, Pierre Barré comes across a notice written by Hervé Chabaud, editor of *L'Union*, the Rheims regional newspaper. It is the heading that catches his eye: *L'officier Canadien Eric Brown recherche ses sauveteurs*. Pierre reads the piece and his memory is jarred by the date of June 28, 1944, but in spite of other amazingly similar details, he believes the story must be a coincidence. How could the RCAF pilot in the newspaper story be the same man they'd had in their house that night? How could that officer have survived?

Pierre Barré thinks about the notice in the paper for several days, speaking to his wife about it and continuing to doubt the possibility that this may be the same pilot his father had brought home. Eventually his wife persuades him to pick up the phone and call the editor of *L'Union* in response to the plea for information about that 1944 night.

"Where would we be without the women of this world?" says Elizabeth when I phone to tell her that anecdote.

It is February 2000 when the discovery of my father's rescuers is made. On sojourn at Beech Cottage when the news arrives, I recognize a rare opportunity: I am close enough to France to go meet the people who saved my father's life.

Elizabeth is pleased about my wish to go to Rheims. I am the advance party: if everything seems legitimate, she and Eric will make plans to fly overseas in the summer. This will be the culmination of Elizabeth's wish to "better late than never thank the brave French family who risked their lives in saving my husband."

During a flurry of faxes sent back and forth from Beech Cottage to France over the next few weeks, I learn new details about the story of my father's rescue. I convey this information back to Vancouver with regularity, and although Elizabeth is excited about each new piece of information, Eric seems withdrawn from the unfolding drama. Elizabeth assures me that he appears interested whenever she tells him about the new discoveries and assumes that he is not saying much because of his difficulty with that part of his history. Because of this, we tread carefully as we exhume each new fact, editing some of the finer points in order to protect Eric's memory from too great a shock.

And so much of what I learn must first be filtered through the poor English of M. Chabaud, the newspaper editor and the main person responsible for locating my father's rescuers. M. Chabaud takes great pains to answer the queries I send in poorly written French, and between the two of us, the story of my father's saviours emerges.

M. Chabaud, contacted by Colonel Marszalek of the French military (who in turn was initially contacted by the French consulate in Vancouver), initiated the search for Eric's rescuers by putting the barest bones of the story — all that he was told — in his paper. He received several phone calls and narrowed down the possibility of involvement to three families. But the investigation was hampered by the lack of any physical evidence of where the Halifax went down: unlike other bombers shot out of the French sky, no pieces of Eric's plane were ever discovered. So Hervé Chabaud was forced to go to each of the three claimants to interrogate them, using his journalistic skills of inquiry to ascertain which, if any, of the families may actually have been part of this story.

"*Il faut être très prudent,*" he tells me, then adds: "*Après cinquante-six ans la mémoire n'est plus très fidèle et nous devons être certain qu'il s'agit bien de cette famille.*" Now Eric, who does not want to get too involved in this investigation, is sent a long list of detailed questions to answer. The moment I read my mother's translation of her husband's answers, I see there is a problem. Eric's responses are vague and without any clarifying note that he doesn't remember much of anything about the night in question.

The problem is exacerbated when I learn that the man found as a result of Hervé Chabaud's investigation is only a few years younger than my father. Eric has always maintained that it was a young person who leaned over him in the field that night, a boy of maybe 10 to 14 years, so he immediately refutes M. Chabaud's identification of his rescuer.

"He's too old. He can't be the right guy," Dad says to me over the phone.

What I don't tell Eric is what the editor has written to me: "[M. Barré] immediately recognized your father on [sic] the picture of the flight lieutenant Eric Brown." Shown six different photographs of other pilots lost that same night, Pierre Barré picked out the one of my father right away.

I also do not tell my father what Hervé mentions later to me: "Sometimes the truth of memory is not good after such an experience like your father's." It dawns on me, when Hervé Chabaud makes this telling comment, that he is far more in touch with the reality of what must have happened that night than I am. He is clearly trying to suggest that the night Eric was shot down, the trauma was so great that my father couldn't possibly have registered — or remembered — details such as the ages of those around him during the few hours spent in their care.

And now it occurs to me that Eric may not want Pierre Barré to be the "right" person; that he may not want to get on that plane and travel back so far in order to thank this stranger for his life. It may require too much in the way of painful emotion from a man who does not like to think about that part of his life.

~∽~

In the week before I leave for Rheims, it happens to me too. Though I am looking forward to such a momentous occasion, I am aware of my own increasing withdrawal from the building emotion of the trip. I find myself experiencing a kind of numbness as the incredible synchronization of this story's events dawns on me. Without the intervention of the Barré family, my father would not have lived to experience the rest of his life. He would never have been reunited with his wife, my mother, and I would not then have been born into a life of my own. It is the "there but for fortune" story in its best manifestation.

So this trip becomes, as a friend says on the eve of my departure, not unlike the chance to thank an organ donor for his/her anonymous and invaluable kindness.

The eight-hour trip from Beech Cottage to Rheims is accomplished with a sense of surrealism surrounding every mile. With each transfer, from car to bus to airplane to shuttle, I feel one step further removed from the present, from the ground beneath my feet, until, inside Hervé Chabaud's apartment, struggling to recall my high-school French, I am struck by the humility of this man and his family who have welcomed a complete stranger into their lives, and all for the benefit of a long-forgotten veteran.

On that first night in France I sleep heavily, my dreams full of confused images of French villagers and dogs, and the next day M. Chabaud drives me into the countryside beyond Rheims. We head for the village of Courcy, and when Hervé stops the car outside a modest bungalow, I see the door open and a distinguished grey-haired man proceed toward us.

I am introduced to Pierre Barré and extend my hand politely, but in the few seconds of that mechanical reaction, he reaches for my shoulders, bending toward me in the typical French greeting of friends. Within seconds of his kissing my cheeks, we are both in tears, Pierre Barré because he cannot believe I am the daughter of the man who lay in his family's kitchen so close to death half a century ago, and me because I am beginning to understand where I stand in relation to real life.

"*Si votre famille n'avait pas sauvé mon pere,*" I splutter in my halting French, "*je ne serrai pas içi aujourdhui pour vous remerçier en personne.*"

But he shakes his head, wiping at his eyes, and tells me that he still cannot believe my father lived. We go inside and I listen as this old man tells me the minutest details about my father's build, and gradually I understand that Pierre Barré was indeed there with my father on that night of June 28, 1944. When he opens a bottle of the famous Rheims champagne, I realize it is unlikely that someone would go to all this trouble just to answer a tiny notice in a local paper were he not in fact a part of such a terrible event. We drink a toast to the success of this final mission and talk some more, aided by the poor English of M. Chabaud, about what has happened in the intervening years, and then, again, what happened on that night. An hour later all three of us return to the car and drive the few miles to Berméricourt, the village where the rescue occurred.

In Berméricourt we stand at the edge of a huge agricultural expanse, a field of wheat perhaps ten miles square, and then Pierre Barré walks me toward the wall where his father located Eric. As we walk he tells me that if my father's parachute had landed anywhere else, the rescue could not have taken place. I stare at the horizon, see in the distance another village from where, the older man tells me, Dr. Barot travelled in such haste on that fateful night, and I struggle to remain grounded while Pierre adds how remarkable it is that my father was saved at all, given the proximity of the German forces on the hill in the distance.

He points to a small bump of land in the direction of Rheims and explains that this is where the German artillery was situated that night. I try to visualize the blaze of fire from the long-barrelled guns in the night, the flash of explosion in my father's Halifax III, and then I try to imagine what a 21-year-old pilot must have felt as the severity of his situation dawned on him. After so many successful missions, the possibility of a failed one had probably never entered his mind, despite the increasing number of losses in the RAF Bomber Command.

"*Il était là-bas,*" Pierre's voice comes from behind me as he points at an old stone wall. This is the place, then, that a farmer, his helper and a dog found my father lying helpless so many years ago.

And now all the thoughts that have plagued the mind of Pierre Barré over the past few months are poured out, spreading over and around me as I stand at the edge of this empty field outside Rheims, trying to set the scene for this story. He tells me how the bombers flew overhead every night, how the area around Rheims lies below the flight path of airplanes from English airfields, that even in the Gulf War they were drowned by the shadows of the American B52s en route to Iran, how the constant noise of war could easily have drowned out the cries of a lone pilot, immobilized by injuries and lost somewhere in a foreign field in the dead of night. And then he tells me once again about the severity of the wound, about the exposed piece of bone with its shattered end and the bloodied sinew of muscles, tendons and ligaments, and then he stops and I hear the lump in his throat when he whispers:

"*Si loin de son pays; si plein de la peine.*"

Once again I feel the hot flood of tears in my eyes. It is impossible, here, now, not to feel stunned by the idea that fate — or something to do with it — has played a remarkable role in the lives touched by this event.

With blurred vision, I turn my eyes across the 180 degrees of expansive fields. Though I know the visual memory of this place will remain imprinted in my brain, I want to record the scene for posterity, and so I lift the small camera I've brought, take pictures of the panorama before me.

And now, standing on the edge of that French field alongside two strangers who are joined to me in the way that only the giving of life can do, I have a sense of arrival. In this land so removed from either set of ancestors, I am suddenly poignantly aware of the depth of my roots.

Now I feel grounded, but not by either the English or Canadian geography I once thought of as my two homes. Now it is the seeing of my life through the stories of those others who have brought me to this point of discovery. The blood and courage of the young airman who became my father, the love and loyalty of the devoted Englishwoman who is his wife — these are my roots.

I stand at the threshold of that elusive goal — home — and step forward.